C000146689

THE POLITICS OF CONSENSUS

For the resolution of conflict and reform of majority rule.

He listened carefully to all the arguments, pondered for a moment or two, and then said,

"No, I don't like it."

"Why not?" was the obvious rejoinder.

"Because," said he, the Communist Party chairperson on the local council's executive committee in the Russian town of Kirov, "you cannot predict the results."

THE POLITICS OF CONSENSUS

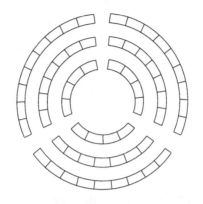

FOR THE RESOLUTION OF CONFLICT AND REFORM OF MAJORITY RULE

by

P J Emerson

"*Consensus Voting Systems*", published in 1991 as a "*samizdat*".
Second edition, "*The Politics of Consensus*", 1994, another "*samizdat*".

ISBN 0 9506028 4 1

Copyright © Peter Emerson, 1994
Rhubarb Cottage
36 Ballysillan Road
Belfast BT14 7QQ

No rights reserved,
for like all good ideas,
they belong to the collective unconscious.

"*This book has received support from the Cultural Traditions
Programme of the Community Relations Council,
which aims to encourage acceptance and understanding
of cultural diversity.*"

Typeset by the author
at Community Computer Resource Centre, Hazelwood College.

Printed by Noel Murphy (Printing), Belfast.

FOR BOSNIA

ACKNOWLEDGEMENTS

No ideas belong to only one person, and for everything in the pages which follow, my thanks must go to the noosphere in general, and then to Dervla Murphy. She it was who encouraged me to tackle this issue of consensus, back in the 70s. The word, I think you'll agree, was not then in vogue.

Of others, over the years, who have helped to develop the methodology of consensus voting, especial mention goes to Phil Kearney of Comhaontas Glas (The Green Party), and to John Robb of the New Ireland Group. Thus, at a 1986 public meeting in Belfast, over two hundred and fifty people came to discuss the constitutional future of Northern Ireland. Nearly all political parties and organisations were involved; those of the cloth met those of the gun; certain members of the Official Unionists sat in the same room with others of Sinn Féin; and together we found some common ground. Further experiments have been conducted in more recent years, with a similar cross section of participants, with the voting procedures computerised, and with even greater success.

To any who might be a little sceptical of consensus politics, therefore, may I suggest that if the latter can be successful in Belfast, then maybe they can be applied anywhere.

Lastly, I would like to thank those with whom I have scrutinised this theme and conducted other experiments in Eastern and Central Europe. How warm were so many to these new ideas, how numerous the editors and journalists who then devoted their columns to this subject... and how strange that some of their counterparts in the western *news* media should persist in their support of the *old* "for-or-against".

In this second edition, the example on pages 110/1 is quoted by kind permission of Oxford University Press. And for their patient proof reading of both words and numbers, I am indebted to Sieneke Hakvoort and Ray Mullen.

CONTENTS

FOREWORD*

When they stop to think about it, it becomes clear to all moderately intelligent human beings that consensus politics is the way forward - the only way forward. Unfortunately most people don't stop to think about such matters. They accept our present form of pseudo-democracy like they accept the weather; it often does nasty things - is inconvenient, even hazardous - but there's nothing anyone can do about it. This of course is partially true; there's nothing any individual can do to change our political systems. But if enough individuals do stop to think about it, and form groups to demonstrate that consensus politics can work, and that the majority of the population want this new system, then something would - eventually - happen.

The snag is that tiny groups, scattered here and there, won't ever rock the pseudo-democratic boat. It is well defended; it has a lot of Fat Cats on board who would quickly become slimmer if consensus politics took off. So mass conversions are needed - and soon, before the myopic Fat Cats inadvertently write FINIS to the story of mankind.

Peter Emerson's brilliant new book, if sufficiently widely read, could considerably speed up the conversion process. It proves that pseudo-democracy is not only obsolete but perilous to the highest degree. And it clearly explains how consensus politics operates. The notion is not just more fall-out from the latest explosion of utopian ideals. It's a practical way of running humanity's affairs and has been used, in some societies, for centuries. It really is workable, if enough people want to make it work.

Read Consensus Voting Systems and encourage everyone you know to read it - and to discuss it and think of ways in which its message might be applied within their own sphere of action. Make people realise that this is not merely another fad, that if we had not been so successfully zombified by our inherited political environment, our instinct for self-preservation would have us all out on the streets NOW, insisting on consensus politics.

Dervla Murphy

* From the first edition

FROM THE BARDS

The arts have always exerted an influence upon the political life of any society, but usually in a rather indirect way. In the experiments on consensus referred to on page iv, however, poets and musicians used their medium to powerful and peaceful effect. For the first gathering, the late John Hewitt wrote and then read the following lines:[1]

THE ANGLO-IRISH ACCORD

These days the air is thick with bitter cries,
as baffled thousands dream they are betrayed,
stripped of the comfort of safe loyalties,
their ancient friends considered enemies,
alone among the nations and afraid.

 And those who now most loudly mouth their fears
 are webbed in spirals of rash verbiage
 which, coarse with coloured epithets, appears
 a rhetoric of cudgels, torches, spears,
 loaded with vivid enmity and rage.

This land we stand on holds a history
so complicated, gashed with violence,
split by belief, by blatant pageantry,
that none can safely stir and still feel free
to voice his hope with any confidence.

 Slave to and victims of this mirror hate,
 surely there must be somewhere we could reach
 a solid track across our quagmire state,
 and on a neutral sod renew the old debate
 which all may join without intemperate speech.

John Hewitt

In another public meeting, Tommy Sands sang this song from his album
"Beyond the Shadows":

1999

Oh IRA and UVF this song is just for you
As you sit down at the table now to see what you can do
At last you've come together after all the tears and time
Sad you didn't do it back in 1969.
History calls you savages but I know that isn't true
For we grew up together and I am part of you
We all had dreams and hopes and fears and someone else to blame
It took so long to realise our dreams were all the same
You know our dreams were all the same but who would dare proclaim
In the anger and the pain our dreams were all the same.
We felt the taste of hunger when the factory went away
And then they closed the hospital they said it didn't pay
And as the rich got richer and they promised us the sky
All we got were promises and coloured flags to fly
I remember well your little girl she had ribbons in her hair
When she came to play that Summer's day with the children in the square
To think they could be here to-day still laughing and alive
If strong men had been wise men in 1979
It was always all or nothing there was nothing in between
Compromise was treachery that's how it always seemed
Well now we're left with nothing but a future we must find
And count the cost of the chances lost in 1989.
Oh IRA and UVF this song is just for you
As you sit down at the table now to see what you can do
At last you've come together after all the tears and time
Sad you didn't do it back in 1999.

Tommy Sands

PROLOGUE TO SECOND EDITION

In December 1992, I went to the former, and future, Yugoslavia. I spent a week over the New Year in Sarajevo, a day or two in the *Bihach* enclave, and then I cycled from Zagreb across Bosnia and on to Belgrade, before returning, again on the push-bike, via Zvornik, Pale, Sarajevo and Mostar.

"A Bosnian Perspective" tells the tale of that journey, but the purpose thereof was to say, on my return to Northern Ireland, that majoritarianism does not work there either! In fact, the visit led me to an even more emphatic conclusion: we need a system of decision-making by which the success of any one policy proposal or candidate should not depend on the votes or even the preferences of only a limited number, (be that number a majority, or merely a large minority). In other words, as in consensus voting, results should be determined by the opinions of all.

Majoritarianism in Yugoslavia

What happened in Serbia, Croatia and then Bosnia can be summarised as follows: the 1989 fall of communism in Central and Eastern Europe led to the emergence of multi-party democracies, everywhere. Hence, in 1990, the various republics of what was still the Yugoslav Federation also went to the polls.

In Serbia, *Miloshevich* knew he needed the support of only a majority; it was, therefore, in his vested interest to discriminate against a minority - he chose the Albanians in Kosova - for thus could he increase his own majority support. (This he had started to do anyway, under the old, one-party system; the introduction of "democracy" changed little.)

In Croatia, the story was similar: *Tudjman* discriminated against his local minority, the Serbs. The effect was twofold: in the elections, he was successful, and he became president; in the *krajina**, he was not, and there he provoked a war!

Lastly, in Bosnia. The adoption of our western party political system led, inevitably, to the division of a people... on religious lines. There soon emerged the Bosnian (Moslem) Party of Democratic Action, the Croatian (Catholic) Democratic Union, and the Serbian (Orthodox) Democratic Party. There was also a League of Reform Forces, founded by *"the last Yugoslav"*, *Ante Markovich*.

Bosnia *"could only have been saved if a political party which spanned the three communities had emerged as the most powerful after the collapse of communist power"*.[2] Well, the Reform League might just have succeeded, for it could well have been everybody's second preference or compromise option. If only the electoral system - but no. Boban and *Karadzhich* came to prominence instead.

One could conclude that in Serbia, the communists won, while in Croatia and Bosnia, they lost. But that fact is irrelevant, and a more accurate summary would suggest that, in the milieu of divisiveness which is such an intrinsic part of the party political system, nationalisms thrived, and won!

A second facet of our antagonistic politics is the two-option referendum. The Croats used one in Croatia and we in the west said that was fine. The Serbs had theirs in the *krajina* and we said that was not. Then, in January 1992, we recognised both Croatia's and Slovenia's independence, but deliberately refused to do the same for Bosnia-Herzegovina, for they too, we insisted, must have a referendum.[3] Thus, though now divided into three, the people

---

* Three "frontier" regions of Croatia first settled by the Serbs as bulwarks against the Ottoman empire.

were given a choice of only two options - two extreme, mutually exclusive options - independence or the *status quo*, (a by now truncated Yugoslavia).

So anyone wishing to vote for compromise was, in effect, disenfranchised, by the democratic process itself! (As was of course the case when the *krajina* of Northern Ireland held its own border referendum, in 1973.)

Lots of ideas could have been discussed and voted on: a UN protectorate, EC membership, a Balkan (con)federation, joint citizenship, joint administrations, the Vance-Owen plan or, better still, some of their own proposals. But again no. Only two options. Whence the Bosnians made what was perhaps their greatest mistake and took one of them, siding with the Croats as it were against the Serbs. On the day of the vote, the barricades went up in Sarajevo. Within days, this once so tranquil land was at war. And within a year, that most unholy Bosnian/Croat alliance had collapsed, in more murder and mayhem.

We cannot put the entire cause of that bloodshed onto a belief in majoritarianism; what we can say, however, is that the Yugoslavs' decision to adopt our divisive western voting procedures was actually the spark which set the Balkan tinders of history ablaze.

Global majoritarianism

Despite it all, the world continues to insist on two-option voting. The Italians reckon they can choose a voting system from a list of only two of them. The Danes think the complicated question of Europe may be reduced to a simple yes-or-no vote, once or if need be, twice. The Irish pretend that emotive issues like divorce and abortion can also be resolved in such divisive polls. While the Russians are totally confused - *Gorbachev's* referendum on the future of the USSR they ignored, the poll on *Yeltsin's* presidency, they had to accept.

And now the European Union wants to adopt the same majority vote, as if it was some ideal. Yet if this practice continues to be the universal norm, and if governments continue to talk of self-determination as if that too must be subject to the wishes of only a majority, there will remain the grave danger of unresolved conflicts in Northern Ireland, the Balkans and the Caucasus, not to mention what may be even more horrific: wars in former communist countries in Central Asia, in multi-racial states like South Africa, and/or multi-ethnic ones, like India. The need for consensus, therefore, cannot be over-emphasised.

The second edition
In the first edition of this book, I argued that we should all acknowledge the validity of our neighbours' legally held aspirations/candidatures and cast our preference points for *all* of them. But that, said some, would be applicable only in an ideal world. Until such is achieved, they continued, and for as long as there are the likes of war criminals standing for election, the democratic process must allow those who wish to participate to only a partial extent, to do just that. I was soon persuaded, for if indeed I were a Bosnian, I too would not want to give any credence at all to the likes of Boban or *Karadzhich!*

The result is this much revised second edition. The main addition relates to the partial vote, but I have also included an historical analysis, as well as a much more detailed critique of some other voting procedures.

Peter Emerson
Belfast, 15.2.94

DEFINITIONS

A - SOME CURRENT VOTING/ELECTORAL SYSTEMS
Majority Voting and "First-past-the-post"
This is the simplest procedure ever devised and can be used for either the selection of a policy or the election of one person. When there are two options or candidates, success depends on the greater number of votes, the simple majority. If there are more than two, victory may sometimes be achieved by only a largest minority.

Proportional Representation - Single Transferable Vote
PR-STV is used for the election of a number of persons in multi-member constituencies. The electorate shall vote 1 for the candidate of their first preference, and they may vote 2 and 3 and... for some or even all the other candidates of their 2nd/3rd/... preferences.

Candidates with more than the necessary quota shall be deemed elected, and any surpluses shall be transferred to other candidates, as per all the 2nd/3rd/... preferences cast. Those with the lowest scores shall then be eliminated, and their votes shall also be transferred. The process shall continue until the required number of candidates has reached the quota, and these too shall then be deemed elected.

Alternative Vote
This is a PR-STV type system for resolving a policy decision or electing just one person. All vote 1, 2, 3... as above; votes cast for the option/candidate with the lowest score shall be transferred as per the 2nd/3rd/... preferences; and the process shall continue until the eventual winner gets 50% + 1 of the valid vote.

Condorcet

Here too, those concerned shall vote 1, 2, 3... and hopefully for all the options/candidates listed. Pairs of options/candidates shall be examined in turn, so if, in a three option/candidate contest, A is more popular than B, B more popular than C and C less popular than A, then A shall be deemed the winner.

B - CONSENSUS VOTING SYSTEMS

Preferendum

[a development of Preference Score or de Borda]

The *"preferendum"* is another linear multiple-choice procedure in which

a) either there shall always be at least 3, usually from 6 to 10, and seldom more than 12, options or candidates;
   or there shall be an open number of candidates, limited only by the size of the constituency;

b) in his/her own order of choice, the voter shall cast preference points *for (one, some or at best) all* the options or candidates listed;

and

c) all points cast by all voters shall be totalled, and the successful options/candidates shall be those with the highest scores.

Matrix Vote

The *"matrix vote"* is a tabular multiple-choice procedure in which the voter may not only cast preference points for those candidates whom he/she wishes to be his/her representatives, but also state in which posts he/she wishes each to serve.

As in the preferendum, all points cast by all shall be taken into account.

C - CONCEPTS

Majoritarianism
A *"belief in, or the existence of, rule or decisions by a majority vote"*.[4]

Pluralism
"Also, the belief that power should be shared among a number of political parties; the toleration or acceptance of a diversity of opinions, values, theories."[5]

Polylogue
An exchange of opinions involving three or more persons.

Consensus
The *"general consensus"* on any one issue is that which is perceived to be the agreed opinion of an overwhelming number, though there may be some who dissent.

A policy decision taken *"in consensus"* is one reached without resort to a "for-or-against" vote. Those concerned either come to a verbal agreement with which none of the participants now dissent; or they vote by using a consensus voting system, and thus find that which enjoys a high *"level of consensual support"* .

This *"level of consensus"* is the perceived or calculated level with which all concerned support a particular proposal or candidature.

In political if not indeed all fora, a level of consensus of 100% is unlikely but nevertheless possible, as when, in a 10-option/candidate poll, all concerned give one particular option or candidate the maximum possible, in this case, 10 points. This does not infer total unanimity of mind on the chosen option or candidate, nor that there are no differences of opinion viz-a-viz the other options/candidates, some of which/whom may also get very high scores. It simply means that all agree either that that policy should be adopted or that that candidate should be elected.

Nota Bene

When using a majority vote, any percentage figures usually refer either to the turnout, those of the electorate who actually participate in the vote, or to the majority/minority who support this or that proposal or candidate. Such percentages therefore refer to numbers of persons.

In consensus voting, a percentage level of consensus refers to the collective degree of enthusiasm with which *everyone* views the option(s) or candidate(s) in question.

So the phrase "a 60% majority in favour" tells us that in a straight two-option vote, 60% voted for, and 40% against. In most circumstances, such a result would be considered a bit of a landslide.

If an option or candidate gets a "60% level of consensus", however, this means that the question was resolved in a multi-option vote, and that all who participated in the democratic process support this particular option or candidate with a level of consensual support of 60%. As we shall see later on, such a measure of overall popularity is not particularly high, and most consensus decisions will enjoy a far greater level of widespread acceptance.

"The full and complete definition of a citizen is confined to those who participate in the governing power."

Aristotle

"A necessary condition of legitimate government is that it be limited in the permissible exercise of political power."[6]

Jules Steinberg on John Locke

CHAPTER 1

INTRODUCTION

M any politicians use the word 'democracy', as if we already have it. But as we all know, the concept is more honoured in the breach than in the observance. Democratic Croats, Democratic Serbs. Social Democrats, Democratic Unionists. The word is used with abandon.

But do all who sing its praises dream of only one form of government, that which is *"of, by and for" all* the people? Why, then, is nearly every so-called democracy unique, each with its own electoral system and internal power structures?

For any given society, the very choice of electoral system means that quite different persons will be elected; secondly, the particular power structures which these persons then inherit will allow them to make very different decisions. So not all such systems and structures can be called 'democratic'.

A few local and/or national variations in rituals and routines are of course both justifiable and desirable. Certain principles, however, should be universal, and these should surely be laid down in an international convention.

Let us start with the dictionary definition. This tells us that a 'democracy' entails *"a form of society which favours equal rights... and tolerance of minority views"*.[7] So any system of government which operates under majority rule, even if it does provide for certain minority rights, cannot be truly democratic. For those minority rights will always be less than equal, especially when it comes to decision-making.

Needless to say, the politicians currently in power do not want to dilute their powers. For this reason, most supposed 'democrats' are loath to be more specific as to just what is, and what is not, democratic. Meanwhile, that which is not democratic, this simple majority vote, is very clearly defined and understood. For without this, they would not be in power.

Admittedly, the procedure used in majority voting is simple; and the outcome, even if subject to a casting vote, is never ambiguous. But it is this very over-simplification of what are usually complex issues which causes all the nonsense of politics, the shenanigans which precede the vote, the bribes and bargains in the corridors of power. No wonder everything is so damned complicated, if not indeed corrupt. While in many circumstances, the consequences of it all are very, very sad.

They include:-

the practice of vote-swopping or "log-rolling" as some Americans call it;[8]

the Unionist shady deals of both Labour and Tory governments whenever their majorities in Westminster are a bit shaky;

the "horse-jumping" of Germany's Free Democrats who were thus able to stay in power for so long;

the bizarre situation in *Dáil Éireann* when a minority of one, Tony Gregory, became the king-maker;

the play-acting in Russia's new parliament where if the minority failed to register, they could thus render the Congress inquorate!

And so it goes on. An endless tale of division and bitterness, the politics of confrontation.

This sometimes reduces the democratic process to little more than a farce. Elsewhere, in Northern Ireland and Yugoslavia for example, it leads to tragedy and bloodshed.

THE BOOK

The text

The purpose of this volume is to describe a better system of decision-making, one which may be used in every forum, from the tranquil gathering of Quakers, to the stormy parliaments of elected representatives. I concentrate on the latter, for if the rules of consensus can survive the machinations of politicians, they will certainly work well in a Friends' meeting house.

The text therefore covers the essential precepts of a democracy, from elections, to debates in chamber, to the final decision-making procedure. But because the methodology used in decision-making governs both the debate and the election, I have decided to discuss this most important item first.

Accordingly, after a short criticism of majoritarianism, chapter 2 stresses the importance of consensus, and explains the theory of how it can be achieved. Chapter 3 gives a brief comparison of the consensus vote with just a few other relevant systems. While the next two chapters cover the "preferendum" as it is called in some detail, apropos both the count and the analysis of the vote, but only in so far as it all applies to the resolution of policy.

The voting system now fully described, we are ready, first, for the methodologies of the debate, chapter 6; for the election which precedes it, chapter 7, where again we discuss the preferendum as well as the matrix vote; and then for the election campaign which is where it all starts, chapter 8. This is followed by a more general section, looking first at one possible consequence of consensus voting, the probabilities of power, before chapter 10 discusses the history of the preferendum. Lastly, after a brief glimpse into the future, chapter 12 returns to the present with a summary of recommendations for immediate implementation.

The appendices

A full understanding of consensus politics may be gleaned from the text alone, though of course, a more comprehensive knowledge may be acquired from the book in its entirety. Because the joys of mathematics are attractive only to a few, however, I have kept most of the examples and any other additional complications to the notes and appendices.

If and when the reader wants to put a particular aspect of consensus politics into practice, he/she need only consult the relevant section. Those wishing to resolve some business or other with a preferendum, for example, having first had a look at chapters 4 - 5, should then examine the detail of appendices 1 - 3. Similarly, anyone contemplating the matrix vote should read the relevant section of chapter 7, and then appendices 6 and 7. The two appendices in between, 4 and 5, are relevant to both voting systems.

Finally, in appendix 9, the reader may compare in some detail the relative attributes of the various voting/electoral systems mentioned in the text.

CHAPTER 2

THE SPIRIT OF CONSENSUS

J ust as in the more traditional 'democratic' structures, so too in consensus politics, people can still voice their own opinions and cherish their own beliefs. They can still argue their corner with all the fervour and passion at their disposal. And they can still enjoy the cut and thrust of controversial debate, in the very best sense of that phrase. The main difference in consensus politics is simply this: there shall never be some outright winners with the rest outright losers. For instead of a two-option vote in which the outcome is the *more* preferred option of only the greater number, there shall invariably be a multi-option poll to find the *most* preferred option of (almost) everybody.

Consensus has been a vital part of many human relationships for years, of course. It is, or should be, a part of every home. And it ought to be a part of every gathering, be it on the streets, at work or at play. No-one should insist on only his/her own point of view; each should be able to participate; and all should accept the final agreement. Alas, as we know, such is rarely seen in parliaments and councils. When power is the prize, those involved tend to split into two and both sides then struggle to win that power, fighting each other with words, or worse, and joining together in consensus only when fighting a war abroad.

  War, however, must be regarded as an *irrational* form of behaviour. Political leaders resort thereto when they feel all *rational* attempts at resolving the particular dispute have failed.

After that, it's win or lose, no compromise, victory or defeat, winner takes all and loser gets nought.

But it is exactly these phrases which also define our so-called democracy: people resort to a vote if all else has failed; thereafter, it is for-or-against, no third opinions, and the stronger side takes all to then dominate the weaker.

Not only does the theatre of war resemble the political scene, as Clausewitz did suggest,[9] but so too do the two sets of actors. Both generals and politicians take sides, and each then talks of the mutual exclusivity of his or her case, so suggesting that the other side's opinion is a diametric opposite. In so doing, they rule out any compromise.

What's more, if someone else comes along to present a third opinion, the two combatants may well unite in a combined opposition thereto. The logic is easy enough: each side claims it is right and the other is wrong, so the very existence of a third point of view might suggest or even prove that both are mistaken.

Sometimes, of course, a third opinion is more to one side than the other. In which case, the other is delighted by that which appears as a split in the former's ranks. Indeed, he might actually encourage same, befriending this new political opposite to thus weaken the original one.

As in war, so too in politics, an enemy's enemy is a friend. Such was the case in 1933 when the German Communists refused to co-operate with their political rivals-cum-neighbours, the Socialists, and thus they helped their opposites, the fascists, come to power. It was all a result of dogmatism, of certain individuals insisting that only they were right, of these and their supporters always thinking in terms of only two supposedly mutually exclusive opposites.

Unfortunately, such unjust and unjustifiable behaviour, such illogical and unnatural division, such "political schizophrenia"[10] is the norm. But it need not, and need never be so! Let me take just two examples, one local, the second global.

There are many who say that Northern Ireland must be *either* a part of the United Kingdom, *or* a part of a United Ireland, inferring if not stating that the first proposal mutually excludes the second. Would it not be better to put the question in a different way, like this: should a 6- or 9-county Northern Ireland be administered by, devolved within, federated with, independent of, or integrated into (the nations of) Britain and/or (the Provinces of) Ireland? That's at least ten proposals already, and not one of them mutually excludes all the other nine. There is much in common, for instance, between a UK-type devolution and a United Ireland-type federation, and it is called a semi-autonomous Northern Ireland!

In any true democracy, the people and/or their representatives should be allowed to express their views, not just on two diametric opposites, but on all the other options as well. In which case, the one which gets most support would almost certainly be regarded as "a most sensible compromise".

Such is not to be, yet. The Northern Ireland problem persists, and largely because of a belief in majoritarianism, a belief which makes neither rational nor intuitive sense, but one which nevertheless dominates nearly all national parliaments, be they of the old one-party states or of our western 'democracies'.

The second example refers to an argument which very nearly led to the annihilation of all life on this planet: communism versus capitalism. The two, we were told, were mutually exclusive. Yet both believed in the super-power politics of a bi-polar world; both believed in armies, nuclear bombs and military industrial complexes; both ran highly centralised economies, the one where the politician ran the nation's business, the other where the business executive became the politician; and both believed in majoritarianism - *Khrushchev* out-voting his 'anti-party group', Thatcher likewise dismissing her opposition; (and it is interesting to remember that the majoritarians of our western capitals led an endless tirade against the Bolsheviks of Moscow, without ever realising that the word 'majoritarianism', on translation into Russian, comes out as, yes, you've guessed it, *'bolshevism'* - although the latter has come to mean other ghastly things as well).

In a broader sense, both the USSR and the USA were European-run, male-dominated, anthropocentric societies based on materialistic philosophies and motivated by greed. They thought they were both so different, yet they were as alike to each other as was to himself *Dostoyevsky's Golyadkin.*[11]

Those questions - are you British or Irish? communist or capitalist? - should never have been posed in that form. To do so was at least unwise, for such infer that differences there may be but of similarities there are none. Which is manifestly untrue.

A more satisfactory approach would consider these similarities as well, for thus could be found the common ground or that which could well be its equivalent, the average public opinion. And just as, among any group of people, there will always be an average height, for example, so too, on any subject under the sun, there will always be an average public opinion, even if no one person actually represents that exact height or opinion.

Take anything you like - arranged marriages, capital punishment, mixed education - public opinion thereon has changed with the passing of the centuries. Accordingly, on any particular subject, there existed at any one time a certain average opinion, and there now exists another. The historian claims to be able to estimate what it was; surely any contemporary observer should have the means with which to calculate what it is, and with a much greater degree of accuracy. Furthermore, in any true democracy, this latter process should be central to every issue.

But we cannot calculate the average height of a group of people by asking them only a two-option question: are you small or tall? Similarly, we cannot estimate an average opinion, simply by asking a two-option, for-or-against type question. It is mathematically impossible, especially if the answer has to be either one or the other. The conclusion is as stark as it is simple: as suggested on page 1, the for-or-against vote is actually undemocratic; it gives a result which is favoured by only some of the people, a *"particular will"* of only a faction in society, the supposed majority.

We must therefore devise a more sophisticated methodology of collating and analysing human choices. To be truly democratic, we need to be able to establish what is *"the general will"*[12] of the entire electorate. The task is formidable. We must allow all who wish to participate, to do so. And we must then estimate, as best we may, the average opinion, collective will or common consensus, of everybody.

It can be found in one of three ways: either by talking and talking until eventually an agreement is reached; or by talking... and then voting, in a consensual ballot; or again, in more extreme circumstances, by all concerned just stating their proposals, and moving straight to a multi-option vote.

In the first, all-talk scenario, success will be achieved only if all concerned accept the need to co-operate.   When proceedings commence, certain proposals may already be on the table. As the debate gets under way, new suggestions will be aired, and maybe, if the level of debate is high, one good idea will lead to another. Eventually - and the whole business may often take rather a long time - a composite and compromise resolution will get maximum support, 100% level of consensus, perhaps. Some, no doubt, will be *delighted* with the outcome; a few may feel it is only *a step in the right direction*; one or two may reckon *it goes a bit too far*; yet others may regard it as *a tolerable result in the circumstances*. But all now agree to accept it.

Such unanimity of mind, we know, is rarely seen in any political forum.   So whenever the passions are high, the subject matter controversial, the attractions of power too great, or simply the level of debate very sophisticated, the above procedures may not work; we should therefore employ the second approach: talk and then vote, or if time is short and/or the mood tense, the third method, vote only.

Again, all participants must accept the need for a certain amount of co-operation. And just as the majoritarian democrat rejects the use of violence and agrees to abide by the final for-or-against vote, so too in consensus politics, all are obliged a) to reject both the force of arms and the force of numbers, and b) to abide by the result of the consensus vote.

Accordingly, everything must be done in any talking phase to ensure that the debate remains a multi-option discussion and does not descend into a two-option argument. This can be achieved by stating, right at the beginning, that at the very end, the decision will be subject not to a two-option vote, but to a multi-option consensus poll. In any civilised conversation, many will be the points of view; and in any compassionate decision-making process, many will be the options.

If come the vote, everyone expresses their opinions on (one, some or better still) all the options listed, we will be able to ascertain which suggestions are felt to be divisive, which are seen as very bad ideas, and which are regarded as really rather sensible. As in the calculation of any average, the more who participate, the better, no matter how tall or small their views. Furthermore, in expressing a viewpoint, each shall affect the average, i.e., each shall make a contribution. And even in such conflict situations as sadly still exist in Northern Ireland, it should be possible to achieve a result which enjoys, not 100% consensus, mind, but a level of consensus of, say, 75%. Indeed, as we shall see, we need never go for less.

If, in debate, everybody is aware that all suggestions will be considered, (all, that is, which do not infringe some agreed norm like the United Nations declaration on human rights), then may a better atmosphere prevail. Furthermore, if the decision is not to depend on the stronger of two sides, there need not be just a dialogue with two opposing factions, but rather a mature "polylogue" of many points of view.

It all depends on the decision-making methodology to be used at the end of the discussion. Let us now, therefore, look first at how the vote proceeds, and only then shall we return to examine further the nature of the debate.

CHAPTER 3

THE VOTE

I n consensus voting, then, I do not vote against. Instead, I only vote for, and ideally for all the options listed... in my own order of preference, of course.

Thus, in a ten-option preferendum (an example of which is given in appendix 1), I give 10 points to the option I like the most, and I may give 9 to my next favourite, 8 to my third choice, and so on, as I wish, all the way down to the end, with 1 point for the option I like the least.

In other words, in completing my ballot paper, I may express a point of view on all the options, and thus may I recognise the validity of other persons' opinions. No longer do I vote *against* you, thereby hoping to outnumber and then dominate you. Rather, I join with you in the knowledge that my and your and everybody else's opinions will all influence the average and to an equal extent. I have my aspirations, and you yours. Let each and everyone of us give full vent to our opinions; in a word, express an opinion on (one, some or) all the options listed; in another word, give an accurate measure of our overall point of view. And then let us seek our common ground or collective wisdom.

In a two-option referendum, the electorate is able to vote in just one of two ways, for or against, A or B. In a three-option preferendum, however, there are six possibilities: ABC, ACB, BAC, BCA, CAB and CBA. Similarly, in a four-option ballot, there are twenty-four different ways of voting, and it all proceeds by happy mathematical progression until, in a ten-option poll, over three million different opinions or emphases may be expressed; (please see page 102).

If we wanted to calculate our average height, we could measure all our individual heights to, let us say, the nearest centimetre. That would give each of us over two hundred different heights to choose from, and that should be good enough. Political opinions are obviously a lot more complex, but a range of three million viewpoints should be sufficient... especially in Northern Ireland where we have only as many opinions as we have people, a mere million or so.

This may all sound a little complicated. It is. May I just repeat, however, that there is a danger in simplicity, and such can be seen in the simple slogans of war! Secondly, we were all born different, and any political system which tries to negate these individual differences may be irrational, unnatural, and unworkable. Thirdly, such a ten-option vote is no more complicated than a pools coupon or an insurance claim. And lastly, it empowers all who participate, for each will actually affect the result.

AN EXAMPLE
Before proceeding further, let us here consider a simple example of a multi-option vote, and see how it works under the various systems mentioned in the definitions: majority voting, alternative vote, the Condorcet system and a preferendum vote.

The simplest example of all multi-option ballots is of course a 3-option poll, so let us take a case in point, that which the Scottish Nationalist Party has proposed[13] - a vote on Scotland's constitutional position between the three options of *status quo* (S), devolution (D) and independence (I). We may assume, I think, that those who vote first for S would prefer D to I for their second choice; that those who most want I would similarly prefer D to S; and that those who most favour D might be split as to their second preferences. And just to keep it really simple, let us hypothesise that the entire Scottish electorate consists of just eleven people, who vote as follows:

	Jill	Joe	Jane	Jock	Jack	Jude	Jan	Jim	John	Jay	Jake
1st choice	S	S	S	S	I	I	I	I	D	D	D
2nd choice	D	D	D	D	D	D	D	D	I	S	I
3rd choice	I	I	I	I	S	S	S	S	S	I	S

Majority Voting

Well, under straight majority rule, the score is S 4, I 4 and D 3, so nobody wins. And because majority voting so often fails to produce a result when there are more than two options listed, the politicians concerned invariably limit both their own and our choice to one of just two alternatives.

Now if, in the above vote, Jack had managed to persuade Jock to vote first not for S but for I, then I would have won, with a relative majority of 5, a "majority" of 45%! There again, if Jock had persuaded Jack... and majority voting is all too often prone to the whims of a few floating voters. Indeed, in some if not most instances (see page 114), the vote is actually determined by those who know or care least about what is going on - as was the case on 28th March 1979, when the fate of a British premier, James Callaghan, was left in the hands of a disinterested Irishman![14]

Alternative Vote

Under AV, with that first round score of S 4, I 4, D 3, D would be eliminated and the three votes of John, Jay and Jake transferred in accordance with their second preferences: 2 to I and 1 to S. So I would win with a score of 6, a real majority of 55%. So at least AV usually gives a (sort of) majority decision.

There again, if Jack had persuaded Jock... or Jock Jack. Or, to take a much more likely occurrence, if Jake the devolutionist had not bothered too much about his second/third preferences, if he had voted DSI and not DIS, the result would have been not I beats S by 6 to 5, but S beats I by the same margin. So, though a great improvement on majority voting, AV may also produce some pretty extraordinary results.

Condorcet

In the Condorcet system, we consider each of three pairs in turn: S and D, D and I, and I and S.

Well, only 4 prefer S to D, but 7 prefer D to S. This we may write as D > S by 7:4. Similarly, D > I by 7:4, and I > S by 6:5. So overall, D is the answer, a result quite at odds to that produced under AV. What's more, Condorcet is a little more stable, for if Jake vacillates on his preferences, or if Jack or Jock persuades Jock or Jack, the overall result stays the same.

A Preferendum

In a preferendum count, we add up all the points cast for all the options. S, I and D get 3 points each for all of 4, 4 and 3 first preferences; 2 points each for 1, 2 and 8 second preferences; and 1 each for 6, 5 and 0 third preferences, respectively. This means they get 12, 12 and 9 points, plus 2, 4 and 16, plus 6, 5 and 0; that is, S, I and D get totals of 20, 21 and 25 points. So again, as in Condorcet, D is the most popular option. And if Jack Jock cajoles Jock Jack, or if Jake is still uncertain, the result again remains unchanged.[15]

On balance, therefore, at least in this example, Condorcet and the preferendum give a much fairer result. There is, however, a significant weakness in the former - the so-called cyclical majority - which will be discussed in appendix 9. Let us here therefore proceed with another specific advantage of the preferendum.

PARTIAL VOTING

There may be those who, for reasons personal, religious or whatever, do not wish to give even 1 point for certain options. They should nevertheless be facilitated to participate in the democratic process to the maximum extent they feel able.

Those who do hand in only a partial ballot, however, shall exercise only a partial influence on the result. Let us look at an example and compare a family of voters:

If in a 10-option ballot, dad gives 10 points to his favourite C and nothing to any of the other options; if, in a word, he says something about C, but nothing, nothing, nothing... about anything else, his vote could be interpreted mathematically as:

$$1 + 0 + 0 + 0 + 0 + 0 + 0 + 0 + 0 + 0;$$

accordingly, it will be recorded as 'C 1' to mean that 1 point goes to C, and, in effect, he will exercise only:

1 point.

If mum annotates two options, giving 10 to her favourite C and 9 to her next choice G; if, therefore, she says something about C, something less about G, but again, nothing, nothing, nothing... about any of the others, her vote will be recorded as

'C 2, G 1', and she will exercise:

$$2 + 1 = 3 \text{ points.}$$

If the son votes for three options, with 10 for C, 9 for G and 8 for J, his vote will be recorded as:

'C 3, G 2, J 1', and he will exercise:

3 + 2 + 1 = 6 points.

While if their daughter gives not only 10 to her favourite C, but points various to all the other options listed, her vote will be recorded like this:

'C 10, G 9, J 8, ... D 2, B 1', say,

and thus she will exercise the full:

10 + 9 + 8 + 7 + 6 + 5 + 4 + 3 + 2 + 1 = 55 points.

This may sound a little unjust: dad exercises just the 1 point, the consensual daughter all 55; but look at it this way:

If you vote for just	1	option,	your favourite will get	1 point;
If you vote for	2	options,	your favourite will get	2 points;
If you vote for	3	options,	your favourite will get	3 points;
and so on.				
Accordingly,				
if you vote for all	10	options,	your favourite will get	10 points,
			the maximum.	

So your influence upon the options you vote for will thus be in direct proportion to the degree of your participation, which sounds fair enough; and for a more mathematical proof of it all, please see appendix 4. In consensus voting, therefore, all partially completed ballots will be recorded as above - please see the guidelines detailed in appendix 4, and these should be outlined in the instructions on the ballot papers, as in appendices 1 and 6.

In all, only those who hand in a completed ballot paper will exercise a full influence. Herein lies a great advantage of the preferendum: unlike the alternative vote and at total odds to majority voting, consensus voting never allows the extremist more influence than is his/her proportional due - (though please see appendix 9).

Meanwhile, those who do exercise only a partial vote, those who do not give any points to option B, say, may rest in the knowledge that B will therefore be less likely to get an overall 75% level of consensus. Such 'anti-B' behaviour will nevertheless be countered by the fact that they will not be able to effect a full 10 points to their favourite C. This suggests that those who want their own choice to be judged the most popular will have a greater chance of success if they are prepared to vote for (some or) all the other options, and to thus indicate (at least a few) which they would be ready to tolerate. In a word, their own best interests lie in their own willingness to compromise (a little).

There may well be some occasions when, for the very best of reasons, a few citizens or elected representatives may choose to abstain, as in a rather obscure debate of which they feel they have insufficient knowledge. This they may do, in the hope or indeed knowledge that the collective wisdom of everybody else will nevertheless be sound. The absence of just a few, in consensus voting, will probably not greatly let alone adversely affect the average opinion. In majority voting, though, as the late Frank Maguire would confirm,[14] the vote of only one can sometimes completely reverse the result!

A summary

In preferenda, each voter uses the language of numbers to express his/her point of view on (one, some or) all the options listed. When talking and talking, it is often the louder men who speak the most; in consensus voting, however, all may exercise an equal influence on the final outcome which, for the moment at least, shall remain unknown.   First comes the count.

CHAPTER 4

THE COUNT

The calculations involved are really quite easy: for all valid full or partial votes, we first add up all the points cast for each option; we then express each total as a percentage of the maximum possible score; and we thus obtain (in a 10-option preferendum) ten levels of consensus.

That's it.

More mathematics, the theory of it all, you will find in appendices 2 - 5. And less you'll find in practice, because all these sums will be done on a computer.

As a voting procedure, therefore, the preferendum is not too difficult to understand. How strange, I thought, when first I published on this theme,[16] that others had not thought of this before. But stranger still, as we shall see in chapter 10, they had.

CHAPTER 5

THE ANALYSIS

L et us assume there are 100 voters, and that each casts a valid full vote in a 10-option poll. If exactly 50 of these voters give their 10 points to a certain option C, if no-one gives it any 9s, 8s, or 7s, or... and if all remaining 50 give it only 1 point, such an option will get 500 + 50 = 550 points, or a level of consensus of 55%. In consensus politics, such mean scores do not add up to much, so option C will fail. It would not have helped much, either, if the figures had differed but little: if (a "majority" of) 51 had given it 10 points and 49 their 1s, it would then have got a total of 559 points or a 55.9% level of consensus.   That, too, would not have been enough.

Such an option we can describe in three different ways. In diagrammatic form, it looks like this:

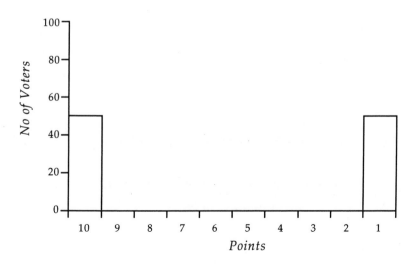

In mathematical terms, as we've already said, it has a level of consensus of only 55%. And in words, well, it is obviously extreme, divisive and aconsensual.   On all three descriptions, therefore, option C is seen to lack any genuine broad-based support.

If, on the other hand, many (let's say 40) give a different option G their 10s, several (30) give it their 9s, some (20) their 8s, a few (10) their 7s, so nobody gives it anything less, then G is probably much more successful.   We can paint it like this:

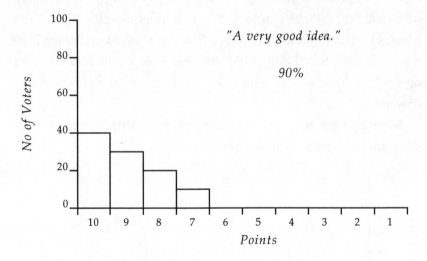

Mathematically speaking, we might add that it enjoys a

$$\frac{(\text{total number of points received })\ \times\ 100}{\text{maximum possible}}$$

$$= \quad \frac{(40x10 + 30x9 + 20x8 + 10x7) \; x \; 100}{1000}$$

$$= \quad \frac{(400 + 270 + 160 + 70) \; x \; 100}{1000}$$

$$= \quad \frac{900 \; x \; 100}{1000}$$

= 90% level of consensus.

While verbally, we can say it is an excellent suggestion.

Actually, I am rather tempted to quote myself (see page 10) and describe this result by saying that some are *"delighted"* with it, a few feel it is *"a step in the right direction"*, one or two that *"it goes a bit too far"* perhaps, and others that it's *"a tolerable result in the circumstances"*. And what some had originally described as enjoying 100% consensus, is actually seen to warrant just 90%.

For a comprehensive analysis, it is advisable to draw all ten diagrams, and basically they fall into five categories.

Something like the above "90 per-center", a curve falling from left to right, could be called *"a very good idea "*; and the higher the starting point along with the steeper the curve, the greater the level of consensus.

Others are as follows:

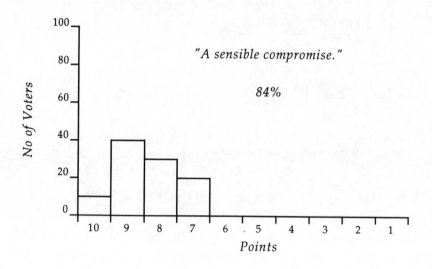

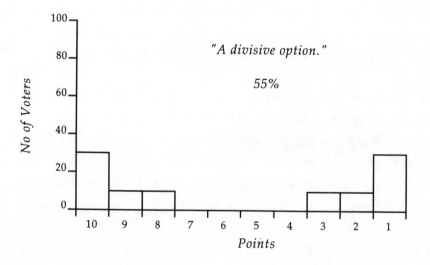

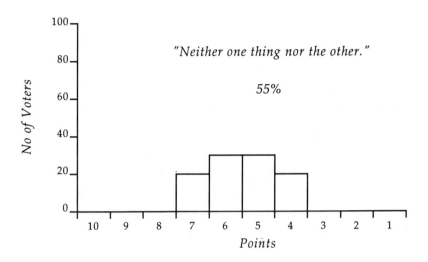

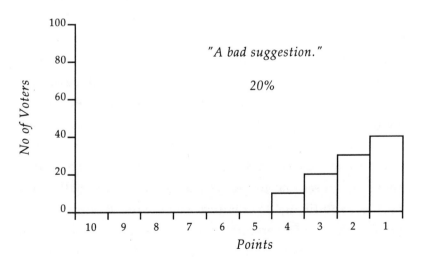

Such a comprehensive analysis can certainly do no harm; at least it will show us more clearly how we all think, and at most, exactly how we feel about the final outcome.

People sometimes just assume that a decision has been taken in consensus, yet who is to know, especially in those rather long-winded debates, what has actually prompted the final agreement. Was it a coming together of minds, a sense of common purpose, or perhaps some ulterior motive; was it a feeling of increasing frustration, or in the more extreme cases, just the requirements of the bladder? And what in fact was the real level of consensus?

Resort to a consensus vote may well be the wiser course of action, therefore, for this will mean the entire democratic process can be completed that much more effectively and accurately.

The consensors and the chairperson
In domestic, industrial or political conflicts, it is always best to rely on at least one impartial referee. So, too, in many political disputes, there is a need for independent arbitration.

As usual, a non-voting chairperson shall be in overall charge of the meeting, but there should also be a team of say three elected and equally independent "consensors". In any debate, the mechanisms of which we will discuss in the next chapter, their job shall be threefold: to decide which proposals comply with the UN declaration and which of these best represent the debate; secondly, to choose the consensual voting system with which the matter may be resolved; and finally, to adjudicate on the result of that vote.

If one option gets a very high level of consensus, 85% or so, it must *ipso facto* be way out in front, so it may be deemed the result. If, however, the subject is more controversial, maybe no one option gets such a high total and instead, two or three options get roughly equal levels, 65% or thereabouts.   If so be it, the consensors will first take the most consensually popular option; next they will examine any other consensually popular options to see which parts thereof may complement the first; and then they will draw up a composite policy to thus make a coherent amalgam. Politics, after all, is the art of compromise; consensus voting is simply its methodology.

In principle, much as this may upset some politicians, there is absolutely nothing wrong with compositing; and perhaps, everything right.

Let us think mathematically again.   If the task is still to calculate that average height, we first ask all to submit an exact measure of themselves, and I think we decided the nearest centimetre will do.   You are lm 73 perhaps, I'm a little lm 59, a third is lm 62, and so it goes on, thousands of different measurements; we just bung all this information into a computer, and out comes an answer, accurate now not just to the nearest centimetre, but depending on the number of participants, to one or two places of decimal: 1 metre, 64.67 centimetres, precisely, a mathematical amalgam.

Compositing is simply a necessary part of any accurate average estimation, and the more who participate, the greater the degree of accuracy of that composite.

Levels of consensus

It must be emphasised that the term "level of consensus", as it relates to any given option or composite, applies to the overall opinion of everybody, or at least of everyone who voted. It does not, I repeat, refer to the number of people who favour that option or composite.

A level of consensus for any one option or composite of options may be defined as that average degree of support which that option or composite enjoys with the electorate as a whole.

Now 100% consensus for any one option is easily understood; it means that in a 10-option poll, they all give that option their 10s. So too the minimum level: if everyone returns a fully completed ballot, and if they all give only 1 point to a particular option, the latter then 'enjoys' a level of consensus of just 10%.

But what does 75% consensus for a particular option signify? It does not infer that 75% of the voters give this option their 10s and 25% their 1s.[17] What it does suggest is that the collective enthusiasm of everybody is either a little muted and/or a little varied.

It may mean, for example, that 50% (of the people) give it their 8s, and 50% their 7s, for that would signify an average score of 7.5, and a level of consensus support (amongst everybody) of 75%.

There again, maybe 25% gave it their 9s, 25% their 8s, 25% their 7s and 25% their 6s, for that too would signify an average of 7.5.

Or again, 50% 10s and 50% 5s would also produce the same 7.5, and this time, we see, opinions are somewhat divided.

Our last example portrays the worst possible division for this given level of consensus: if 72.2% gave this option their 10s, and 27.8% their 1s, the level of consensus would yet again be 75%.

A true understanding, therefore, will be possible if the relevant histograms are displayed, and only then should the consensors embark on the final adjudication of the vote.

Compositing the result

Let us now, therefore, take a second look at the principles of analysis in a little more detail, and this time I will choose the recent British controversy over what, if anything, was to replace the rates.

Well a good debate there would never be, if everything was seen in terms of only two options - "poll tax or the old system?" - but that is exactly what happened. So third and other opinions rarely got a decent hearing. If consensus had been the norm, all the little subtleties and nuances of different policies could have been discussed, and voted on, in a sensible and civilised way. The corresponding ballot paper could well have contained the following six options:

	O P T I O N	Points	
A	The old rates system.		
B	A poll tax or community charge.		*A*
C	A local income tax.		*6-option*
D	Local council discretion.		*ballot*
E	Site value rating system.		
F	Property Tax.		

If option D, for example, local government control, had got a very high level of consensus, local control it would have been; if it had got a low level, central government control would have been required; and if the level had been rather average, any local control could have been subject to certain central government ceilings. The two forms of control were not mutually exclusive; and compositing was not only possible, but desirable.

Secondly, if both option C, local income tax, and option E, site-value rating, had got roughly the same high levels of support, any future rates could have been determined both by the residents' incomes *and* by the value of their site.

And so on. Rarely should any one option have been seen as mutually exclusive of another. The result would doubtless have been a composite policy consisting of those options which had received good levels of consensual support; and even though this too was a very divisive topic, such a combination could well have enjoyed a level of consensus of 75% or more.

Shopping list

On some occasions, the result will consist of a number of options, as when a group of people makes a collective decision on a "shopping list" of items. A question like "which six newspapers shall we have in the common room?" for example, can best be answered by all concerned first listing their six favourites in order, and then by adding all the points cast to see which six have the highest totals. In such an instance, a consensual vote might take just a minute or two, but a debate on this topic would last all day!

Perhaps I should add at this stage that which may well be obvious: the greater the choice, the more likely will be found a near exact average and therefore a successful common consensus.

If there are but three options, two of them might be extremes, and the remaining one a very poor compromise. In this case, results will be at best confusing. If, however, there are between six and ten options, some may be divisive, others extreme, a few rather weak, but (as we said on page 7), at least one will come to be seen as "a most sensible compromise".

Two theoretical examples of how people might vote, and of how such voting patterns might then be interpreted, are given in appendix 3.

CHAPTER 6

THE DEBATE

So we now know how the debate will end: all will agree on matters uncontroversial, while on any contentious issues, either later or sooner, they will resort to a consensus vote.

But how shall the discussions begin?

Initially, no doubt, there will be a number of motions before the house or certain specific items on the agenda. In either case, from a simple study of the subject and a cursory glance at any theoretical compromise options, the consensors shall draw up a list of points to be considered. Thus, to return to our example of the constitutional future of Northern Ireland, they might display a list of about ten options, such as in appendix 1, with perhaps re-partition and UN arbitration thrown in as two further items worthy of consideration. As the debate proceeds, one or two points may be agreed upon, a few ideas dismissed unanimously, but most issues hotly contested. Furthermore, other factors may be raised, new suggestions made, and so on.

Accordingly, the consensors will initiate, maintain, and gradually finalise a list of all disputed points, so to form one or more preferenda of distinct policy options. This too it is best to display on an overhead projector or computer screen.

It will no doubt be possible to resolve some issues with just the one ballot; more complex topics, however, may require the consensors to summarise the discussion under a number of subject headings. Let us assume here, though, that one will suffice.

The old and the new

In many debates of the more traditional variety, a motion is put to the house, an amendment perhaps is proposed, and speakers both for and against then produce their various arguments, supposedly in an effort to persuade their opponents. At the end of the day, however, no matter how brilliant any ideas which may have been inspired by and proposed during the course of the debate, everyone returns to (an amended version of) the original motion, and casts a vote, for-or-against.

So one could say that there is little point in debating at all, especially if every participant has already made up his/her immovable mind or if, in other words, it's "a party issue".

Consensus politics, in contrast, allows the debate to develop, and sometimes in a way which as it were must be unpredictable, at least for those involved. For why else would they meet? Some politicians might object to such a characteristic, but any political scientist should surely applaud this uncertainty, as long as such a debate can be successfully and unambiguously concluded, which is indeed the case.

As mentioned above, the consensors usually produce an initial agenda, just to establish the multi-faceted nature of the topic in question. By the end of the debate, though, their final preferendum may bear little resemblance to the original list, especially if the debate has been constructive, literally, and this is all the more likely if that first list was a fair one.

The balanced debate and the vote

The preferendum must of course be balanced. In the Northern Ireland case, this means that some options should reflect a British dimension, others an Irish one, a few both perhaps, and maybe one or two neither. It all depends on the debate itself. If one new idea is similar to one already listed, the consensors may choose to combine the two. If another new idea is quite different, it might upset the overall balance, and cause others to be changed a little. Thus, even in preparing a preferendum, a certain amount of compositing may be unavoidable... or again desirable.

Balance, it must be stressed, is important, for much depends on the (exact wording of the) options listed. In a 2-option referendum, though, literally everything depends on (the exact wording of) only one question! Which rather suggests the politicians currently enjoy a monopoly of power, while the people can act only as a rubber stamp.

In 1993, for example, the Italians had a referendum on which electoral system they were going to use; they rejected most of their old list system*, and thus adopted the even more antique majority vote. But because the question did not even mention PR-STV, they could not have had a good debate, they certainly did not have a good vote, and still nobody knows what they really would have liked. If only they had had a preferendum, with all voting systems listed, doubtless a more accurate measure of Italian public opinion could have been realised.

Let us go a little further. Such a ballot paper might well have included everything from the (British) first-past-the-post, via the (German) additional-member-system** and a (Danish or Swiss) list

---

* There are, in fact, several varieties of the list system, and the best one is in Switzerland. Basically, each party proposes a number of candidates; voters choose in some systems one name, in others more than one; and proportionality overall is effected by a "topping up" process, as in:

** the additional member system, a combination of majority voting in each constituency, plus nation-wide "topping up" to achieve proportionality between the parties.

system, to the (Irish and Maltese) PR-STV or even to (as yet, no one nation's) consensus voting. The final result would probably have been something from the middle of the list, a compromise if you like.

And we can again surmise that the answers obtained in (undemocratic) referenda will invariably be different from those obtained in preferenda.

There will undoubtedly be those occasions when certain persons will dispute the consensors' judgement. In our chosen Italian example, the majoritarian lobby would probably complain about the inclusion of all those PR-type options. But so too, any old Stalinists would object to the inclusion of anything but a one-option vote!

The consensors must ensure that, prior to the vote, the debate remains multi-optional, and how many PR-type voting systems should be included on the final ballot will depend, as suggested earlier, on the participants' various proposals.

Eventually, of course, the UN charter might well rule that all electoral systems shall be proportional, in which case the western Bolsheviks would not get their 'take-it-or-leave-it' vote listed, just as those old Soviet Bolsheviks wouldn't get their 'take-it-or-take-it' vote.

In all circumstances, however, at the end of the debate and before proceeding to the vote, the chair should run down the proposed preferendum, just to ensure all fair points have been covered, either verbatim or in composite.

The task of the consensors, like that of any referee, is unenviable... but also, in this game above all others, absolutely essential.

The Lights

The structure of debate

Consensus in debate can be further promoted by a few simple techniques, many of which are slowly becoming more popular.

It is better, for example, for all to sit in a circle, tiered if necessary, and on convening, for a moment's silence to be observed. A set of "traffic lights" is also recommended, the timekeeper switching to green when the chair asks a new speaker to start, to amber when 30 seconds remain, and to red when his/her fair share of time is exhausted. Only the most stubborn will need further prompting from the chair.

Ideally, these lights will be positioned in the centre of the circle. A second light, shaped in the form of a question mark and placed on top of the traffic lights, should be at the disposal of the consensors. If, then, someone says something which might be construed as insulting and/or inaccurate, the consensors may use this light to thus "question" these remarks. So all will know the offending remark has been detected; the noise will have been challenged by a light; and no-one else need object.

In such an instance, the chair will ask both the speaker to stop and, if need be, the consensors to say why they decided to interrupt. The point made, the speaker will then be asked to explain or retract the remark, as required.

The particular phrase may well have been just a slip of the tongue. On other occasions, I have seen political adversaries trying to criticise and misquote each other with slur and slander. Yet in all circumstances, the light has worked well; and sometimes, the very fact that it's there tends to encourage both self-restraint and mutual respect.

If at any time a session does get a bit out of hand, the chair may call for another moment of silence and suggest that all should reflect on the purpose of the meeting. If the rumpus gets really serious, he/she may ask everyone else to quietly stand and join hands, to thus acknowledge that common purpose. And if the disturbance still persists, then maybe it is best for the chair to adjourn. Albeit limited experience suggests, however, that such measures will rarely be necessary. Given, what's more, that all reasonable proposals shall be included into the final preferendum ballot, few should have cause to complain.

One additional point also deserves our attention. As we saw in the analyses, the result will be determined by an accurate measure of *all* opinions. So if in a debate of say 8 options, somebody wants a particular policy to be adopted, he or she must persuade not only the mild supporter to become more committed, to give 7 or 8 points instead of just 5 or 6, but also the opponent to warm a little, now to give 4 or 5, perhaps, instead of just 1 or 2. Thus there is more to be gained, not in preaching to the converted, but in gently wooing those who, in a majoritarian milieu, would be seen as political adversaries.

Furthermore, the proponent of any one policy will have a vested interest in its non-exclusivity, and he or she will wish to show how it could enhance, or be enhanced by, some or all of the other options.

Thus the very use of a consensual system will in itself promote consensus, both in the course of a civilised debate, and in any resolutions which may follow.

WILL IT WORK?

If the final vote is susceptible to any form of abuse, the debate itself will all too easily deteriorate. Politics always was a dirty game, certainly some will try to "fix" the result of any preferendum, and a determined lobby could attempt to do this in two different ways:

a) by getting all their supporters to vote according to one particular pattern, or

b) by persuading some of them to vote tactically.

a) Manipulation by 'a majority'

This applies both to the resolution of a policy question (as in chapter 5), or to the election of representatives, (which will be discussed in the next chapter). A more detailed description is in appendix 9, but briefly, it's like this:

Imagine a 10-option ballot in which some of those listed are of one particular ilk, and 51% of those voting also belong to that ilk. If, then, this majority votes *en bloc* for only its own, the remaining 49% will not be able to influence the result at all! The answer will be either the adoption of one or a composite of two or more options, and all of that one particular ilk. Which is exactly what happens in a majoritarian procedure. A preferendum cannot be any worse.

In the Northern Ireland context, with a balanced preferendum of four solely British options, four solely Irish and two other, a regimented majority of 51% could almost guarantee their favourite would be the most popular. In such instances, however, these tactics would show the supposedly most popular options enjoying levels of consensus only slightly above the average, and well below the required 75%. That's the theory. And in practice, given the chance of acting in a more sophisticated way, surely no society would ever split into only two extreme camps, the likes of Sinn Féin and the DUP#? Northern Ireland is proof positive enough, and just as the use of PR-STV allows for the very existence of the Alliance Party, for example, so too the introduction of the preferendum will also cater for a less polarised society.

b) Tactical voting

In most cases of tactical majority voting, people tend to 'forget' their most favoured option (or candidate) and to vote instead for a second or third choice, so to defeat an undesired 'opposite'.

In consensus voting, however, where we vote only for, and where we influence the score of (one, some or) all the options/candidates listed, any attempt at tactical voting against a supposed threat is almost bound to fail.

They can try, of course, and doubtless they will. In a 6-option poll, for instance, they could ask all their supporters to hand in a full vote with a 6 for their favourite and a 1, not to their most detested choice, but to what they suspect is actually more likely to get the highest level of consensus. If, for example, the Unionists feel that a Federal Ireland might prove to be the most popular, they could ask their supporters to give that option only a 1. Their chances of persuasion, however, could well be slim, for the committed loyalist will hardly give more points to that which he regards as an anathema, the United Ireland option, and less to his considered lesser evil. They could, therefore, go for a partial vote, but that we know will reduce their own chances of success.

\# Democratic Unionist Party, extreme Unionist.

Life, in other words, will be difficult, and meanwhile the press will be asking questions on all the options listed, and those in power will be expected to talk of which they will vote for and with what preference, and of which they will boycott, and why.

What will be both possible and likely is a certain amount of "tactical voting for". Some might choose to give fewer points to that which they feel is both their own and many others' favourite, and more to a less popular second choice. Doubtless, in such circumstances, the voter will be reasonably content with either outcome.

When first devised, the "preferendum" was open to some abuse, for those who voted partially were still able to exercise the maximum number of points for their favourite *and* to ignore all the other options/candidates. No wonder M de Borda, a retired matelot turned mathematician whom we will meet again in chapter 10, described 'the preferendum' as being suitable *"only for the honest"*.[18] Now, however, given that the partial vote shall have only a partial influence, given the requirement for a 75% level of consensus, and given the possibility of a composite result, the "dishonest" will no longer be able to dominate the proceedings and the preferendum will *"yield a unique finest outcome in the overwhelming majority of cases"*.[19]

A summary

Those who favour majority rule are those who benefit from it, politicians in the main whose only constituency is a section of society, their own supporters. If they then criticise the preferendum because it might be abused by a majority, they may well be compared to the dictator generals who first bemoan their fragile democracies, and then arrange the *coup*!

We human beings are all subjective creatures, responding to divisive forces if such indeed prevail. We are nevertheless capable of change. And we ourselves can determine that which then determines us! To devise a divisive system is to risk division; to use a cohesive methodology at least offers hope.

Accordingly, we may now suggest that especially in lands of conflict and bitter memories, the best voting procedure is the preferendum. If indeed the debate will end with such a decision-making process, if in other words all the participants know that they can actually influence the final outcome and that that outcome will be a compromise at least partially in their favour, then may the debate itself be constructive and civilised, if not indeed inspirational.

This methodology should therefore be introduced into those lands where peace prevails, and as a matter of the utmost urgency, for the only argument offered in favour of majority rule in Northern Ireland hangs on its continued use in Westminster! Meanwhile, in lands divided, this same preferendum should be an integral part of the peace process, and it must be stressed that the term embraces the debate which precedes the vote, the vote itself, and the consensors' analysis.

CHAPTER 7

ELECTIONS

W hether we are choosing policies or people, be it in chamber or in the country at large, the same spirit of consensus should apply.

So again, none of us need vote *against* our fellow human beings. Instead, we may cast our preferences *for* (one, some or) *all* the candidates listed, thereby recognising the candidature of each. In other words, we may vote for (almost) everyone, regardless of their age, sex, colour, religious belief or... well, read on.

As we saw earlier, a degree of compromise can be guaranteed in all matters of policy by allowing the consensors to adjudicate as necessary both on the options listed and on any subsequent composite. A similar degree of compromise can be maintained in matters of representation if elections involve the appointment of more than one person, e.g., both the chairperson *and* a vice-chair and/or a chairperson elect.

Accordingly, in consensus elections, we shall always elect two or more persons, and there will therefore be at least three candidates, usually rather more.

Consensus voting can be used on all the following occasions: -

A) when we the *electors* choose   (i) our representatives,

and/or   (ii) our executive; or

B) when they the *elected* choose (i) their representatives or

executive,

and/or   (ii) a sub-committee.

A(i) Choosing our representatives
- by Preferendum

In both local and general elections, the council area, region or country, shall be divided up into multi-member constituencies, most to send from four to six councillors or parliamentarians to the relevant forum. In this respect, so far, it is all rather similar to PR-STV.

If the number of candidates is twelve or less, the corresponding ballot paper shall be similar to that shown in appendix 1. Again, the consensors must ensure the final list is balanced, if need be by limiting the number of candidates in terms both of gender and of party affiliation. All named candidates shall be allowed to describe themselves and/or their party in a limited number of words; and the instructions will differ but slightly from those shown in the appendix; (again, I choose the example of a ten-candidate ballot).

"Write a 10 opposite the candidate whose policies you like the most; write a 9 opposite the candidate whose policies you like second best..." and so on.

Needless to say, in a three-seater constituency, the three candidates with the three highest levels of consensus will then be deemed elected.

In the event of a tie, the candidate with the greater number of 10s (to stick to our current example) will be the successful one; if they are still neck-and-neck, we will look at their 9s' totals, and so on.

If one of the chosen few then dies or resigns, the consensors will just refer back to the original ballot papers, transfer any preference points cast for the deceased in accordance with the voters' intentions, and do a re-count. (It is worth pointing out that bye-elections are only a part of an obsolescent system in which those who hold or aspire to power seldom seek a compromise.)

In societies where the accepted voting system is PR-STV or the preferendum, then, as it were by definition, there should never be any mid-term bye-elections - unless, perhaps, there has been a re-call - see page 73.

When there are more than twelve candidates, listing all of them may be a little impracticable. In such circumstances, it is therefore better to hold two rounds: in the first, each voter shall choose, in his/her order of preference, just four candidates, giving 4 points to his/her favourite, 3 to his/her next preference, etc.. We add up all the points cast for each candidate and select the ten most popular ones.

These then enter a second round ballot, and as long as the number of candidates each voter is allowed to choose in the first round is less than half of the number listed in the second ballot paper, this second list will be balanced, as it were automatically. In this second poll, as in the above ten-candidate preferendum, each shall vote for (one, some or) all.

It must be emphasised that we would never wish to see a second round in which only two participated; such, alas, is our present system, if we are French, for example. If there were twenty candidates in the first encounter, then let there be a full ten in the second, for that will allow for a fair degree of proportionality (or compromise) in the results.

Elections consisting of two rounds, however, will probably, be a rarity. Indeed, in a really consensual democracy such as we'll consider in the next chapter, two-tier polls need never occur.

A(ii) Choosing our executive
- by Preferendum

If our parliaments so decide, we the constituents may have one set of elections for the legislature, and another for the executive. Indeed, if we live in the USA, that is exactly what we've got.

As suggested above, however, we shall never elect just the one person; as an absolute minimum, we shall choose both a president *and* his/her vice, and better still if we are able to select yet other members of the president's council at the same time. So, to stick to the USA for the moment, if Clinton is the most consensually popular candidate, he will duly be president; but if, in the same election, Jackson is the second most popular, then he will move into the White House as well.   The two will then have to work together, just as their multi-racial electorate must live together, and to this theme we shall return.

B(i) Choosing their executive
- by Matrix Vote

We, the electors, choose a parliament; and parliament, if it so wishes, may then "choose" its executive or government.   Such is our unhappy majoritarian lot, if we are British or Irish. So a better system...

First, though, if I may, I'll digress.   The for-or-against vote and the x-vote are, in effect, point decisions.   There is a choice of perhaps only two alternatives, and each voter is required to opt for just one of them.   It is, therefore, a very limited decision-making process, and a very primitive one too.   In PR-STV perhaps, and in the preferendum definitely, we progress from a point decision to a line of information.   And as shown on pages 12 and 102, the corresponding degree of choice is that much greater.

A further logical step is to move to the second dimension, the page; and when any elected body chooses its executive, the best method is the matrix vote which, unlike the preferendum, has definitely not been invented by any one else... as far as I know.

For the sake of simplicity, let us assume that all concerned have decided, in consensus, to elect a government consisting of only six ministers: a premier, a deputy, and four ministers of peace, health, tax and land.

Each member may then choose, in his/her own order of preference, six names, each to serve in one particular post. These he/she shall list on the ballot paper as shown, writing only one name in each column and, at the same time, only one in each row, six different names in all. (For details of both the vote and the count, please see appendices 6 and 7.)

	Please enter your choice of names here below					
	6pts	5pts	4pts	3pts	2pts	1pt
Premier						
Deputy PM						
Min of Peace						
Min of Health						
Min of Tax						
Min of Land						

The Matrix Vote - a 6-post ballot paper

The list of candidates shall include every member of parliament or council, the only exceptions being those who have already served a term or two. Or maybe it is better to list just those not eligible for election, lest the very fact of listing leads to unnecessary hustings and hustlings.

In smaller gatherings, when a committee of ten is electing an executive of six, say, or even when a committee of six is deciding who shall do which job, the list should include those not eligible for office, and those unwilling to serve in certain specific posts.

The result, the common consensus of our elected representatives, will be the six candidates with the most points, and each will serve in the post to which, in the consensus of those voting, he/she is most suited. And they too will then work together.

It is worth pointing out that such a democratically elected executive would, in fact, be a form of power-sharing, all-party coalition, government of national unity, round-table co-operation or call it what we will, depending on whether we are Northern Irish, Bulgarian, Israeli, Polish, or whatever. Some earlier examples of such did not work too well... but that was partly due to the fact that many of their participants continued to believe in majoritarianism. Consensually elected fora (or any other for that matter) will be able to function effectively, if they do so in consensus.

B(ii) Choosing their sub-committee
- by the Modified Matrix Vote

If a sub-committee is to consist of a chairperson, a deputy and, say, four ordinary members, we may assume that everyone attaches equal importance to the first-named posts. In which case, a modified matrix may be used, and the basic layout thereof is as shown opposite.

I need hardly add that the candidate with the highest score will take the chair, the runner-up will be the deputy, and the next four also-rans will join as members. And these six will also work together. There again, members in cross-party sub-committees normally do.

Points	Post	Please enter your choice of names here
6	Chairperson	
5	Deputy Chair	
4	Ordinary Member	
3	Ordinary Member	
2	Ordinary Member	
1	Ordinary Member	

The Modified Matrix - a 6-post ballot paper

A criticism

The one inherent disadvantage in the matrix vote and the modified matrix is that the voter need only choose a limited number as opposed to (one, some or) all of the candidates. So the bigot, if tempted, could doubtless opt for only his own. (And we are all bigots, to some extent anyway; I for one am an anti-nuke fanatic, and as for my views on majoritarianism...)

If the danger is real, perhaps the best approach is to vote in two stages, just as the electorate might if and when there are more than a dozen candidates (see page 43). Such a danger may be regarded as minimal, however, if the number of ministers to be elected is sufficiently high, i.e., greater than ten. Furthermore, it may well disappear altogether when the party system of politics is not the rigid set-up that it is to-day.

In such an ideal situation, people will appoint someone to a certain ministry on account of that person's suitability, and in the matrix vote experiment referred to in the acknowledgements, the local Belfast councillor chosen to look after the health chair was a doctor, and whether he was God-fearing, and which God he feared, was apparently of little concern.

Sub-committees tend to be smaller, but as there are usually quite a few of them, the approved list of candidates for any one sub-committee will invariably be relatively short. Thus the bigot will run short of like-thinkers. Just in case, though, it may be wiser for everyone to choose all the subcommittee chairpersons in a matrix vote, and then to use modified matrices to choose their members.

An overriding advantage of these two matrix voting systems is that they offer our elected representatives the maximum amount of choice, so their deployment is therefore advisable. The question as to which voting system shall be used on which occasion shall remain, as always, with the consensors. For the politicians shall decide what to do and who shall do it; the consensors will merely tell them how they shall make these decisions.

A comparison

Of electoral systems currently in use, PR-STV has the advantage of allowing for the representation, not only of the majority, but also of any sizeable minority. Proportionality was not, however, an inherent feature of the original Borda system, though the consensus principles which distinguish the preferendum will invariably ensure the latter does possess this quality.

As we saw in chapter 6, this proportionality of the preferendum is not immediately apparent, neither to the punter nor even to the mathematician; and PR-STV has a number of serious defects, of which more in appendix 9.

In conflict situations, therefore, where people may still need the security of "their own", the most practical electoral system is probably a combination of the Borda system and PR-STV called Quota Preference Score or QPS, (please see page 69).

When choosing a government, some parliaments such as those in Britain and Ireland allow the prime minister or *taoiseach* to have almost complete control. At the same time, these premiers talk of power-sharing for Northern Ireland! The very least they could do, in their search for a solution to this problem, is to practice what they preach. Accordingly, they should allow parliament to elect its government, either by PR-STV or by QPS, or best of all by the matrix vote. Again, all countries at peace should reform their own systems of government, and as quickly as possible.

Only one detail is in doubt: either we the people elect a legislature, and it then chooses its executive; or we elect, in two separate votes, first the one and then the other.

On balance, I think I prefer the former routine. The executive therein will consist of democratically elected persons, whereas separately elected presidents, be they Russian or American, have a nasty habit of appointing all sorts of non-elected "advisers". Secondly, what with their presidential councils and so on, these executives have tended to become mini-legislatures as well. Thirdly, we seem to elect the same sort of people no matter what the election. And lastly, the legislature's consensually elected executive will consist of a good number and, as we saw earlier, the greater that number, the greater the degree of fairness.

So if millions elect hundreds, and these hundreds then elect a score, proportionality will be maintained, and the government will represent all the people, and not just (less than) half of them.

CHAPTER 8

THE ELECTION CAMPAIGN

I n most current elections, a certain psychological thought process works like this: *I* vote for what *I* want; I hope there will be more of me and less of you... and you? Well, by the sound of some of those campaign slogans, you can go to hell!

In effect, the x-vote almost forces us to be selfish; PR-STV allows us to be consensual if we want to be, but it still permits the dogmatic to be intransigent; the preferendum, however, asks us all to be consensual, as of right. No-one is forced to compromise on his/her principles, and each, if they so prefer, may hand in only a partial vote. But all are asked to compromise with their neighbours. The word, after all, has two meanings, and both encapsulate ideals.

Now because the present systems are in effect orientated towards selfishness, all politicians are at least tempted to play on this emotion. Some exploit our feelings of greed, and we have all heard those promises and seen those pre-election budgets; others, even worse, exploit our fears. In Northern Ireland again, many an election campaign has been marked by heightened violence. In Britain, the Falklands (Malvinas) war led to a "khaki election". While in the United States, in nearly every post-war and pre-*Gorbachev* presidential election, the he (and sure, it was always a he) who was the more belligerent, was invariably the winner. So the US democratic system was actually a part of the arms race!

A further consequence of our divisive political system suggests it is easier for candidates to try and persuade the electorate, not that they are right, rather that their opponents are wrong. Hence many an election is littered with charge and counter-charge, and one accuses the other of being weak, an appeaser, and God knows what besides. Hence again those nasty slogans - defeat this, no to that, smash the other - it is all the language of war. Literally everything takes on a negative air; and people vote, not so much *for* a policy let alone a philosophy, more *against* a supposed opposite.

The eventual result is really quite frightening. For *"all tend to become what they first oppose"*.[20] And just as one football team, though totally against its opponents, is nevertheless utterly dependent on them, so too, in the two-party political system, the one is invariably dependent upon the other. For otherwise there would be no game.

The DUP opposes, but benefits from the existence of, Sinn Féin. Labour often complained of, but itself helped to create, its supposed opposite of Thatcherism. Similarly, if he fails to curb his extremism, the anti-fascist may all too readily himself become a fascist.

As often as not, differences between the parties are figments of the political imagination. But in any majoritarian system, politicians are invariably tempted to oppose, either the others' policies if not indeed their personalities. They create, and then benefit from, division. *"Because [they] had governed ill, it was put in [their] power to govern worse, and liberty was undermined, for fear it would be overthrown."*[21]

As Ketcham suggests, these words could easily apply to President Nixon, while to-day we might add *Yeltsin*, let alone *Tudjman* and *Miloshevich*. They were actually written apropos Henry VII, but they describe, do they not, an *"international schizophrenia"*.[22]

In consensus voting, an altogether different psychology is involved. I still vote for my own candidate, of course, but I may also recognise the candidature of your nominee, and I will give him/her at least 1 point, regardless, as was mentioned on page 41, of his/her age, sex, colour, religious belief or, as may now be added, *political persuasion*. If I don't, if I fill in only a partial ballot and refuse to acknowledge a particular opponent, then as we know, I hamper not only his/her chances but also my own.

Candidatures

In days to come, further evolution of our species may be possible. At the moment, many candidates are actually self-appointed, each deciding that he/she is right and all right if not in fact brilliant. Again, it seems, our democratic systems suffer from a bias towards selfishness. Perhaps it would be better, therefore, if there were no candidates at all or, to put it another way, if everyone was a candidate.   In every multi-member constituency of say six representatives, the electorate could choose six names from amongst those there resident, with political position regarded more as a one-off duty, rather like jury service. If such was the case, people might well opt for those they regard as *"unbiased, impartial, just and fair"*,[23] and maybe even the modest would get elected.   In a consensual milieu, they would not feel too far from home, as few would be struggling for power, not least because no one would get it.

The dangers of such no-candidate or all-candidate elections are similar to those mentioned on page 47, namely, they allow the political, religious or nationalist bigot to be so. For the time being, therefore, if but in societies at peace, maybe it is better to progress to the straight forward multi-candidate preferendum in which that same good bigot, if he is to be democratic in the best sense of the word, must cast some points for (some or) all. And we'll move on to the no-candidate system of elections, just as soon as we have a no-party system of democracy.   Which is all in chapter 11.

CHAPTER 9

PROBABILITIES OF POWER

U nder those nasty one-party dictatorships, the probability of the dictator getting it all his own way is literally 1 in 1; that is obvious enough.

In two-party democracies, however, all is subject to the vote. Quite right too. But if, as is usually the case, the decision is based on a for-or-against vote, the chances of any one political leader being able to dominate proceedings are, in theory, 1 in 2. If again, that leader has a majority in the house, the whole damn thing is a foregone conclusion, and his chances of success are the same as those of he whose system he abhors, 1 in 1. Thus, when it came to the crunch, Thatcher was able to steam-roll her poll tax through, just like a petty dictator. She is by no means the only leader so to act, neither in her own party, nor indeed in her country.

So let's now see what the score will be in a consensual democracy, first in regard to a policy decision, then apropos an election.

A - POLICY DECISIONS

If a certain matter is to be resolved in a six-option preferendum, the theoretical chances of any one leader getting most of what he wants are down to at least 1 in 6; if, furthermore, the issue is a very contentious affair and if, therefore, there is a close-run vote, the consensors will be obliged to produce a composite result, and the chances of this hallowed politico having all his wishes fulfilled are probably much less. Which again suggests compositing is a good thing.

B - AN ELECTION
In electing its executive, parliament may use a preferendum, a modified matrix or a matrix vote. Assuming the voters all hand in a fully completed ballot paper, the maximum probabilities involved in each electoral system are as follows, (and for the sums involved, please see appendix 8).

i) The Preferendum
(If they elect just the one person in a six-candidate ballot, the chances of any one person being able to insist on his own point of view will again be just that, 1 in 6. However, as we said earlier, they shall always elect more than one.)

So if they are electing two persons, a chair and a deputy, say, in the same six-candidate preferendum, the chances of any one particular set of results will be 1 in 15.

ii) A Modified Matrix
If our representatives opt to elect a sub-committee of six members from a list of ten candidates using a modified matrix, such as is shown on page 47, the chances of any one leader getting his own chosen half-dozen will be 1 in 210, and if he wants his own personal choice of chair and deputy chair as well, his chances will be even smaller: 1 in 6,300.

iii) The Matrix Vote
As the choice of each voter gets bigger, so too the chances of any one leader being able to dictate proceedings get smaller and smaller. If they now elect a named six-member cabinet from the same ten candidates as per the matrix vote ballot paper of page 45, each will be able to vote in any one of 100,000,000 different ways.

Ipso facto, the likelihood of any one person being able to win everything will be minimal:

- his chances of being able to insist, successfully, on his own chosen six will be as in the modified matrix, 1 in 210;
- if, in addition, he must have so-and-so as his premier, the odds will go down to 1 in 1,260;
- if the old diehard demands his own deputy as well, they will stand at 1 in 6,300;
- and if he rants on about his own particular nominees for all six posts, it will be down again to 1 in 151,200.

Balance of power

No matter which way you look at it, therefore, the chances of any one person being able to rule a consensual parliamentary roost will be greatly reduced.

In effect, consensus spells the end for any personality cults, be they those of the one-party state, *Stalin* and his -ism, or those of the two-party systems, such as are seen in the very existence of words like 'thatcherism' and 'reaganomics'.

Consensus politics will actually allow our democratic institutions to do what they were designed to do in the first place.   The legislature, by itself, shall make the decisions; and these shall be represented and/or executed by its chosen representatives in the executive.   Hence the words.

Secondly, the traditional 3-way separation of powers - in the legislature, executive and judiciary - will be all the more enhanced. The people elect the legislature; the legislature chooses its executive; the executive appoints a judiciary; and the legislature elects from this judiciary its consensors.

A summary

In all, the emphasis on leadership will be much reduced.　The highest authority in the land will be the legislature; and the executive will be mere functionaries, either to implement parliament's decisions or, in natural and/or other emergencies, to be thoroughly accountable thereto.

In a consensual democracy, therefore, no matter what the decision, no one party or leader shall win everything; but (almost) everyone will win something.　So our consensually elected representatives' consensually elected representatives, each so different perhaps one from another, will at last be able to (live and) work together, Clinton with Jackson for example, male with female, Christian with Moslem and Hindu and atheist, each representing the consensual decisions of a parliament in which the interests of each and all are consensually represented.

CHAPTER 10

THE PREFERENDUM - A HISTORY

A s I said in chapter 4, I initially thought I had devised something really rather unique. But in fact, though not then so named, the preferendum[24] was actually invented, oh, years ago. It is just as well, therefore, that my first edition gave all due acknowledgement to the collective unconscious!

The gentleman concerned was a certain Rev. Charles Dodgson, better known to most as Lewis Carroll for his delightful tales of Alice. But the story does not stop or start there, for at the time of his discovery, he too was *"in complete ignorance"*[25] of the even earlier inventions of Jean Charles de Borda.[26]

Like his fellow countryman the Marquis de Condorcet (whose method we outlined in chapter 3), de Borda had realised that 2-option majority voting was *probably* not good enough. As too, of course, had others elsewhere. A contemporary of theirs, Jean d'Alembert, had suggested *"the opinion of the majority is often not the best one"*,[27] a thought which John Dryden had preferred to put in verse:

"Nor is the people's judgement always true,
"The most may err as grossly as the few."[28]

Something better was required, for politics was *"a matter not of the will but of reason; [it was not a] mechanism for expressing the greatest interest of the greatest number* [majority rule], *but the collective vehicle for the discovery and implementation of the truth"*.[29] Such was Condorcet's philosophy, but it was primarily as mathematicians engaged in the science of probability that both he and de Borda devised their new voting mechanisms. Mention should also be made of the Marquis de Laplace who argued for the same counting methodology in the Borda system as that independently devised for the preferendum two centuries later, here in Northern Ireland.[30]

It was a time of amazing social change. The European Americans had just had their revolution, the French were soon to have theirs. And many were trying to escape, not only from the *ancien régime* of the absolute monarch, (a system of national government 'justified' by that concoction called the 'divine right' of kings) but also from what the English had devised as a replacement but which many nevertheless disliked - the constitutional monarchy and a two-party parliament. The latter, they suggested, led to the emergence of narrow political parties (and another fabrication, the 'right' of majority rule).   These then argued and fought with each other. And the subsequent *"alternate domination of one faction over another,"* George Washington declared, *"has perpetuated the most horrid enormities [and] is itself a frightful abomination"*.[31]

Jean-Jacques Rousseau had earlier pursued the same logic to criticise, though he still grudgingly accepted, the very idea of representative government: *"The people of England regards itself as free,"* he had noted, *"but it is greatly mistaken; it is free only during the election of MPs. As soon as they are elected, slavery overtakes it, and it is nothing."*[32]

While *Lev Tolstoy*, with hindsight perhaps but foresight as well, was a little more emphatic: *"In representative government,"* he wrote, *"not only is it possible that power will be seized by cunning, immoral and artful mediocrities, such as various prime ministers and presidents have been, but the construction of those governments is such that only that kind of people can obtain power."*[33] Well, John Major. What more need be said?

Lots. For many have criticised the two-party political system, especially at times of great social upheaval. Yet still it persists. One of Washington's successors, James Monroe, considered *"the existence [of parties] as the curse of the country"*.[34] But, as we all know, the US have still got them! Furthermore, many of their politicians went silent, and the main critics were then their dissident authors: *"From neither party, when in power, has the world any benefits to expect,"* said one.[35]

The Irish also criticised the Westminster style of government. Kevin O'Higgins suggested, *"We'll have groups here [in the Dáil Éireann], small groups of seven or eight. We will not have parties on definite lines of political cleavage."*[36] But, just like those Americans, that's exactly what they have got!

As too, of course, the English. But they also had their critics. John Stuart Mill asked for *"a House of Commons which shall be a fitting representation of all the feelings of the people and not merely of their party feelings"*,[37] while the thoughts of another man of letters, Hilaire Belloc, bring us right back to Rousseau: *"Something alien has intervened between electors and elected, between legislature and executive, something that deflects the workings of representative institutions. That thing is the Party System."*[38]

Perestroika

In more recent years, the world has seen the collapse of that which was definitely a terrible system, the one-party rule of the Bolsheviks. Those who brought about the tumultuous changes were initially a little uncertain as to which political system to adopt instead. (Today, no doubt, they are even more perplexed!) On looking at the two US parties for example, *Gorbachev* was understandably confused: *"there is no particular difference,"* he concluded.[39]

How sad, therefore, that despite advice,[40] he and his fellow Soviets nevertheless decided to adopt that which was the cause of the US sickness, the simple majority vote. How sad, in other words, that they resolved to reform a dying empire via a system in which one 'half' of Congress would have a vested interest in the failures of the other 'half' - and that too is schizophrenic! How sad indeed that *Gorbachev* should thus fall out with his former friend, *Yeltsin*;[41] and sadder still that the latter should then have a shoot-out with his old chums, *Rutskoy* and *Khasbulatov!*

The cause

For so many of these ills, the practice of majority voting is partially to blame. One might also conclude that Marx's original decision to divide the people into two, the workers versus the bourgeoisie, was itself a cause of *Lenin's* and then *Stalin's* labour camps, and the subsequent deaths of 'a minority' of 24 million! Take it further, for was not Marx first prompted by the Hegelian idea of thesis versus antithesis, as if good, a synthesis, could only come via such initial conflict?

Yet the preferendum is a process via which a synthesis may be achieved from a plurality of theses, with little or no bitterness at all. Why, therefore, has it so conspicuously failed?

"Soon after hearing de Borda's paper in 1784, the Academy of Sciences adopted his method in elections to its membership. It remained in use until 1800, when it was attacked by a new member... Napoleon Bonaparte."[42] And that was the end of it. Until the Rev. Dodgson came along, but he unfortunately failed to write the intended book.[43]

So majority rule it is, and for no better reason than divine right it was.

Even in academic circles, voting systems generally were and still are the subject of very little research. When Duncan Black first decided to look into it all in 1958, he *"did not even know it had a history"*.[44] Michael Dummett was equally shocked in 1984: *"The only serious work on the theory of voting had been carried out in France... and subsequently almost entirely forgotten."*[45]

So many nations have produced their critics of majority rule, yet few have resolved to reject that which is its very basis: the 2-option, majority vote.

Why not? Is it because our elected politicians want to retain their monopoly of power? That perhaps is true - inexcusable but understandable if not indeed inevitable. But why do so many journalists and political scientists so seldom question the use of majority voting? It is that which Professor Dummett cannot understand.[46]

Yet reform of our majoritarian system of politics may well be a *sine qua non* of a solution to so many politically motivated violent conflicts. More than anything else, it is a belief in majoritarianism which perpetuates the troubles in Northern Ireland; which prompted the collapse of Yugoslavia; which led to the war in Nagorno-Karabakh; which now tempts South Africa's extreme opposites to campaign in schizophrenic tandem for their own separate statelets - more bloody ethnic cleansing; and which also encourages a resurgence of tensions between the major tribes in Kenya, a conflict which Kenyatta had tried to obviate by the setting up of (that which should have been but alas was not a pluralist) one-party state.

The sorry tale continues, majorities fighting minorities, by word and then by deed. Consensus politics could bring an end to it all, and maybe, one day, it will.

As I said so often in Moscow, the greatest effect of *perestroika* will be felt, not so much in Russia, more in the Western world outside. For no longer will the two-party system be able to point the finger at the communist bloc and claim itself to be good, because the latter was bad. Change, therefore, there will surely be.

Reform of majority rule

There is little wrong in a simple for-or-against vote, if all concerned agree to its use. The question, "Shall we now break for lunch?" for instance, may easily be resolved by a straight show of hands. If, however, the issue is serious, and if the minority should refuse to accept the result of a 2-option vote, the majority shall have no right whatsoever to insist on its enactment. (Nor, for that matter, shall the minority have the right to a total veto.) Thatcher, to return to the poll tax example, may have had a majority (in the House); but she had no consensus for that policy, neither in the House nor in the country at large, and therefore no right whatsoever to force it through.

As a democratic tool, the for-or-against vote is hopelessly out of date. It either leads to division in lands otherwise united, or it exacerbates the tensions in split communities. It might have been adequate, for a time; it was, in its day, a great improvement; but it has served its historical purpose and now it must go! For we all have the right to participate in government. Democracy is for everybody, not just 50% and a bit. Consensus is a human right.

The future

Now for the English parliament to have divided into two opposing camps may have seemed natural enough, for was not everything either true or false, right or wrong, of God or of the devil?

But maybe it is even more natural for people to come together. The most obvious (pro)creative power is inherent in a union of male and female, but there is also an amazing potential to be gained if, for instance, the Western materialist could but learn from the Eastern mystic, or the temperate head understand the soul of the Sub-Saharan tropics. And a real peace will emerge, be it in Northern Ireland or in the world at large, with a coming together of our collective opposites.

A summary

Thus may we conclude that just as there *was* no divine right of kings, so too, there *is* no right to majority rule. Indeed, in any serious dispute, the very use of the simple majority vote may be an infringement of that minority's human rights.

A true democracy should reflect in its legislation the average opinion of all its citizens. Everyone has the right to influence that average opinion in equal measure. So maybe consensus voting is a right too.

We might even suggest the following clause be added to the UN declaration:-

"No decision shall be passed into law, unless it enjoys either a weighted majority of, or a level of consensual support of, at least 75%."

CHAPTER 11

CONSENSUS
AND THE SURVIVAL OF OUR SPECIES

C onsensus politics , I would like to suggest, are directly related to the reform of three aspects of human behaviour which cannot be allowed to continue unchanged.

Firstly, we know the world will not survive unless we stop fighting wars. We must, therefore, resolve all future conflicts peacefully.

This simply cannot be done with a majority vote, especially if one side wants majority rule within *these* borders, the other within *those*, and if both pretend that they have another mythical right, that of self-determination. For no society should be able to 'determine' its 'self', on the basis of only a majority of that self.

In the last chapter, we said that neither side has the right to rule the other, without taking the latter's interests into account. In addition, all national borders are, to greater or lesser extent, artificial concoctions of the human mind. Lastly, each side has a responsibility towards its neighbours. So on all three counts, both sides are wrong.

And maybe it is unwise, even to take sides.

The solution to any conflict will always involve a degree of compromise. In theory, therefore, no matter what or where the tension, the use of a preferendum, and that would include a parliamentary debate or public inquiry, could both facilitate, and be a part of, the reconciliation process. It would be, if you like, the very catalyst of consensus.

Secondly, the world will not survive if we fail to tackle our mounting ecological crises.

Within a majoritarian system, any government in power tends to see everything in terms of win-or-lose, and the most important item on its agenda is invariably the winning of the next election. Hence the short term tax concessions, immediate exploitation of a few more resources, and so on. In a word, the future is often sacrificed for the sake of the present, and a majoritarian form of democracy may actually be a threat to the survival of this planet.

In addition, no majority of western petrol consumers has the right to ignore the wishes of a minority, the Pacific Islanders, for example. To solve such problems as global warming, we really must co-operate.

Thirdly, humankind must evolve. And just as the world progressed from the monarchies of yesterday to the mainly majoritarian democracies of to-day, so must we now move to a more pluralistic multi-party or even no-party democracy.

The kings, alas, were reluctant to reform. To persuade our present day leaders of the advantages of consensus may be just as difficult. Hopefully, however, they will change their minds long before we cut off their heads, and all will be achieved in a much more peaceful manner. For the very existence of the computer makes such an advance inevitable. The two-party system evolved from, and still depends on, the simple for-or-against vote. If everything is a case of *this* or *that,* all too easily will the *this* whip demand that all *this*-party members vote for *this,* because who on earth would vote for *that*? When, however, the abacus is at last replaced by the computer; when, subsequently, all is subject to a six-option preferendum, say, and when therefore it is a question of

720 *"thises and thats"*, the whips will be rendered redundant. In a nutshell, consensus voting will lead to a break-up of the present two-party political system.

Parties may still exist, of course, parties, groups, lobbies and organisations, *"small groups of seven or eight"*, (please see page 59). But they will be free associations, and the formal party power structures we know to-day will at last begin to fade.

Such an evolutionary step forward will in itself promote further evolution. Under present majoritarian forms of government, those inspired by a new idea have to air their views, promote them, round up support... and they will get it adopted only when they have the backing of a majority. If science worked under the same principles, poor old Einstein would still be preaching the proofs of relativity.

Take, for example, the case of PR-STV, first mooted in England over a hundred years ago,[47] and still nowhere to be seen in that realm (except in its church's synod).

In consensus politics, however, any new idea will as it were immediately affect the common consensus, just as a baby child will affect the national average height, the moment it is born. If, furthermore, the idea is a good one and survives the test of time, it will gradually become more popular and, albeit slowly, be incorporated into the system of government.

Consensus, then, is evolutionary, in both senses of the word, an important part of our brave new world...

But it is needed now, for otherwise we may not get there.

CHAPTER 12

EPILOGUE

"**S**imple majorities do not work in a divided society," was an oft-repeated conclusion of the Opsahl inquiry.[48] But simple majorities do not work, full stop. Neither in elections, nor in chamber, nor even in the party system of politics do they work at all well - please see appendix 9.

Furthermore, in Switzerland, it is accepted that *"The majority should not do everything it would be permitted to do... and must do more than required,"*[49] and the Swiss, of course, have long enjoyed a *"system of balanced multi-party government"*[50] with *"PR for political parties on each committee"*[51] and so forth. Elsewhere, though, or so it would seem, majority rule holds sway.

Again I ask why? Why is it that so many people actually believe majority rule is OK? And why *"is the theory of voting... unknown to politicians, to others involved in decision making... to experts in political theory and students of psephology?"*[52]

The Majoritarian Myth and Conflict Resolution

Of those who have studied the politics of conflict, some have chosen to concentrate on the umpteen wrongs of majority voting[53] while others in analysing the mathematical theory of voting systems, have assumed unwisely that all options and even candidates are mutually exclusive.[54]

At the same time, various social psychologists have written at incredible length on conflict resolution but, for reasons which are quite incomprehensible, some of them do not even refer to the conflicts created or at least exacerbated by majority voting, let alone those solved or placated by other voting procedures.[55] Finally, there are those who advocate a rather complicated multi-option voting procedure for use in the world of commerce, as if different criteria should apply in the workplace.[56] They are all, or so it would seem, doing their own thing.

A more interdisciplinary approach is required. And in advocating the voting/electoral systems detailed in this book, I have approached the topic from my own direct experience in the conflict in Northern Ireland, from what I hope is an understanding of human nature, and from a faith in our ideals of democracy and human rights.

The preferendum and the matrix vote are not mathematical devices which allow for 'nice' results. Rather, they are means by which all can exercise their democratic rights to participate with everyone else in their own government. Now the fruits of our collective wisdoms may well turn out to be 'nice' ones. I believe they will. But that will be because of the wonderful invention called us, and not because of any contrived calculus!

So I would now like to summarise those principles on which most collective decisions should be made, and certainly most political ones.

A - REPRESENTATION

Representative parliaments are certainly open to abuse, and all the warnings of Rousseau and others are undoubtedly true, especially if those bodies split into two factions. This they will invariably do, if they choose to take most of their decisions on the basis of a 2-option vote.

In the more primitive two-party systems as in Britain, the two main parties alternate in power, and leave the others almost permanently in a semi-Siberian (bolshevik) cold. While in slightly more advanced multi-party systems as in the Netherlands, elections often precede a period of no government at all, as various parties then wheel and deal to form a majority coalition.

If only such fora would choose to take all their decisions in consensus, most of the ill-effects of factionalism could be avoided, and parliaments could instead enjoy a healthy pluralism, with members divided into *"small groups of seven or eight"*, (page 59 again).

Representative government and representative parliaments are still therefore an ideal, if, that is, they reject the simple majority vote and practice power-sharing. For just as all have the right to be represented in parliament, so too, and *ipso facto,* all have the right to be represented in government. In all elections, therefore, a form of proportional representation is an as yet undeclared basic human right. Power-sharing also involves shared decision-making, post rotation and citizens' initiatives, of which more in a moment or two.

B - ELECTIONS
General

Elections to all fora should be held in multi-member constituencies, most returning from 4 to 6 members, according to the population density of such rural or urban localities. Elections should be held either by PR-STV, or by preferenda, or perhaps by that combination of the two we mentioned, the Quota Preference Score.[57]

This starts like PR-STV, and anyone with a surplus is immediately deemed elected; but then, with no transfers or eliminations, it moves into a variation of the preferendum and step by step, those with the highest preferendum scores fill all the remaining posts. (Please see appendix 9.)

Other forms of PR like the more simplistic list systems or the additional member system are not so good, for they tend to favour and perpetuate the party system of government. Which is why the parties concerned adopted them!

In chamber

Any forum wishing to elect either an executive or a sub-committee should do so using the matrix or modified matrix vote, though in such societies as remain bitterly divided, PR-STV or QPS could be used as an interim measure.

Gender quotas

If in both sets of elections, PR-STV is the chosen system, it may be necessary to establish gender quotas such that, in say a 4-member constituency, two of those elected shall be female and two male. If, therefore, in the count, candidates C and G have been successfully elected and yet both are male, and if the next candidate to reach the quota is also male, his votes shall be transferred in accordance with the voters' subsequent preferences, and the process continued until two females are elected.

In consensus voting, such quotas might not be so necessary. For men are often the more extreme, and *"if [the preferendum] is used, parties of the extremities [will] tend to wither and disappear, while parties of the centre [will] prosper"*.[58] As a precautionary measure, however, and until such time as the world is rather more egalitarian, either the consensors should ensure equal female/male representation on the preferendum ballot paper, and/or as above with PR-STV, equal success in the count.

C - DECISION-MAKING

Majority Voting

Majority voting should be used only if there is a consensus for its use and, even then, majority decisions should be adopted only if there is at least a 75% majority in favour. The logic is clear: if there is no 75% majority, the matter is obviously controversial, so doubtless there is no consensus for a majority vote. Resort should therefore be made to a multi-option process.

Preferenda

On most occasions, those concerned will already know which issues are a matter of some dispute. In these instances, the consensors should immediately insist on a preferendum, without first thinking of a majority vote. If then in a 3-option ballot, no one option gets a 75% level of consensus, (which as we know is quite different from a 75% weighted majority), the debate should be rejoined, the search for other options continued, and a further preferendum held in which more options are listed.

In other words, the degree of controversy in debate will be catered for by the number of proposals raised. In resolving a not very contentious issue like the re-naming of Peter the Great's capital city, the example we will consider on page 112, doubtless all would have been content with a choice of just three: Leningrad, Petrograd and St. Petersberg. Questions of greater import - Scotland's constitution, Northern Ireland's status, Bosnia's future, and so on - will require a longer list of options. But as I say, the degree of controversy will invariably be apparent during the course of the debate, so the consensors will usually be able to choose a sufficient number of options for the final preferendum, and in most cases, only one vote will be necessary.

Thus the preferendum may be regarded as self-regulatory, and this applies as much to debates in chamber as it does to general polls for the entire electorate.

The consensors and the chairperson

To ensure such procedures are followed, it is absolutely essential for all concerned in decision making, and especially those in political circles, to appoint a team of consensors.

When the English devised the parliamentary post of Mr/Mme Speaker, they certainly accepted the need for an impartial chair. But the job is far too complicated for just one person. Accordingly, there should also be a team of consensors to ensure the multi-option debate never deteriorates into a two-option confrontation.

National referenda/preferenda and the citizens' initiative*

"The only referendum which will prove of the slightest value will be the referendum accompanied by the initiative."[59] Such, of course, was first introduced into Switzerland, in 1891. So even the Swiss use majority voting, though maybe they too will soon adopt a multi-option procedure.

Of others on this planet, the only citizens to enjoy both the referendum and the initiative are the Italians and some Americans, those lucky enough to live in 22 of the States. Other countries like Ireland have the referendum without the initiative, but at least it's enshrined in her constitution; while the use of such a poll in Britain is subject only to the will of parliament, or rather the whim of government.

---

* This allows a certain number of citizens, usually measured in thousands, to petition the government for a binding national referendum on any reasonable subject.

In many instances, the above quotation appears to be entirely relevant, for most politicians in power only allow a referendum to be held, when they think they are going to win.[60] Their three main disappointments of recent years occurred with the Danes on Maastricht,[61] the Irish on electoral and divorce reform,[62] and the Austrians on a brand new nuclear power station.[63] It was almost a case of the politicians versus the people, Rousseau might have said, and were not the people right? (Except, of course, the Irish on divorce - if only they too had had a preferendum![64])

So national referenda/preferenda should indeed be accompanied by the initiative. If need be, the vote should be preceded by a debate in parliament or better still, a public inquiry. And the ballot paper should be compiled just as in any other preferendum.

The right of re-call

As with the citizens' initiative, so too any constituency should have the right to re-call any one of its elected representatives, if, that is, a sufficient number of the electorate consider the latter's performance to be unsatisfactory, and if such an opinion is not too strongly opposed by others in that constituency.

Terms of office/post rotation

As inferred on page 45, most terms of office should be limited to a fixed time scale, and maybe it is wise to suggest the number two, as in Ireland and the USA for the post of president. This suggests the incumbent will be tempted to do a good job during his/her first term of office, if only to succeed in any re-election bid.

There again, perhaps such high posts should be rotated annually, as do the Swiss,[65] with terms of office limitations applicable to all other elected posts.

A summary

A consensual democracy should be structured so as to facilitate the peaceful resolution of all political conflicts. This may be done not only by limiting any temptations of power abuse to which elected representatives and especially those in office might otherwise succumb, but also by encouraging that form of collective behaviour which allows for the best possible form of consensus. This happens when, via words alone and/or votes as well, the very meeting of minds finds that excellent idea or policy option, or that brilliant collective wisdom which Condorcet called *"the truth"*.

APPENDICES

"The use of applied mathematics in its relation to a physical problem involves three stages:

i)   a dive from the world of reality into the world of mathematics;

ii)   a swim in the world of mathematics; and

iii)   a climb from the world of mathematics back into the world of reality, carrying the prediction in our teeth."[66]

APPENDIX 1

A Preferendum

THE CONSTITUTIONAL FUTURE OF NORTHERN IRELAND

Write a 10 opposite the option you like the most; write a 9 opposite your next favourite; write an 8 opposite your third choice; and so on, as you wish, (all the way) down to the end, with a 1 opposite the option you like least of all.

If you vote for only 1 option, you will exercise only   *1 point.*

If you vote for 2 options, you'll exercise   *2 + 1 = 3 points.*

If you vote for 3 options, you'll exercise   *3 + 2 + 1 = 6 points.*

If you vote for 4 options, you'll exercise   *4 + 3 + 2 + 1 = 10 points.*

If you vote for 5 options, you'll exercise......   *15 points.*

If you vote for 6 options, you'll exercise......   *21 points.*

And so on.

So best to vote for all 10 options, for then you will exercise full

10 + 9 + 8 + 7 + 6 + 5 + 4 + 3 + 2 + 1 = 55 points.

O P T I O N S	Points
A Northern Ireland to be integrated into the United Kingdom	
B Northern Ireland to part of a unitary state Republic of Ireland	
C Northern Ireland to be devolved within the United Kingdom in an internal settlement	
D Northern Ireland to be in a 2-part federation with the Republic of Ireland	
E Northern Ireland to be a 9-county unit in a 4-part federation with the ancient Provinces of Ireland	
F Northern Ireland to be part of an Anglo-Celtic Federation	
G Northern Ireland to be administered under the joint authority of both Britain and Ireland	
H Northern Ireland to be an independent statelet	
I Northern Ireland to be under direct rule from London, with no Anglo-Irish agreement	
J Northern Ireland to be administered as at present, the Anglo-Irish agreement unchanged	

APPENDIX 2

The Preferendum Count

On many occasions, the count will be done on a computer. It can, however, be done by hand, and to show how it all happens, I have chosen a simple five-option/candidate preferendum, in which just the three of us - you, I and another - take part.

You, let us say, vote like this:	My opinion is:	And another says:
A 1	A 3	A 1
B 5	B 4	B 3
C 4	C 5	C 4
D 2	D 2	D 2
E 3	E 1	E 5

Let us now record your vote. On a computer panel (or piece of paper) it would look like this:

OPTION OR CANDIDATE	THE	VOTES				
CANDIDATE	5pts	4pts	3pts	2pts	1pt	Unused
A					1	
B	1					
C		1				
D				1		
E			1			
Unused						

We may note at this stage that you exercised all your preferences, and you voted for all the options/candidates. Thus the above completed picture shows a 1 in each column and a 1 in each row.

Now we record my vote as well, adding it to yours:

OPTION OR	THE		VOTES			
CANDIDATE	5pts	4pts	3pts	2pts	1pt	Unused
A			1		1	
B	1	1				
C	1	1				
D				2		
E			1		1	
Unused						

and finally, we add another's:

OPTION OR	THE		VOTES			
CANDIDATE	5pts	4pts	3pts	2pts	1pt	Unused
A			1		2	
B	1	1	1			
C	1	2				
D				3		
E	1		1		1	
Unused						

On a completed count of three full votes, every column should add up to 3, as too should every row. If one of them does not, then either the vote was invalid or we recorded it incorrectly... and if such is the case, the computer will bleep bleep.

So far so good; and to clarify the next stage, that final picture is here repeated, though the 'unused' bits, their function completed, have now been deleted.

OPTION OR	THE	VOTES			
CANDIDATE	5pts	4pts	3pts	2pts	1pt
A			1		2
B	1	1	1		
C	1	2			
D				3	
E	1		1		1

Let us now press another button, so to get the points. These we will add up to give five separate totals, each of which we will then express as a percentage of the maximum possible score (in this case, 15), so to get five levels of consensus. Thus a second panel would be as shown, and this is best displayed directly below the one above:

OPTION OR	THE	POINTS				TOTALS	LEVELS OF
CANDIDATE	5pts	4pts	3pts	2pts	1pt		CONSENSUS
A			3		2	5	33%
B	5	4	3			12	80%
C	5	8				13	87%
D				6		6	40%
E	5		3		1	9	60%

Again, each column adds up, and any mistake would be readily apparent.

The result is obvious enough, perhaps, but may I now refer you back to chapter 5.

In just such a five-option preferendum, each voter may cast a total of:

$5 + 4 + 3 + 2 + 1 = 15$ points, and this the mathematician describes as $\Sigma 5$.

In an N-option/candidate preferendum, then, each may cast a total of ΣN points, and if V is the valid vote, the final count can be verified (by the computer) according to the following bottom line:

OPTION OR CANDIDATE	THE	POINTS				TOTALS	LEVELS OF CONSENSUS
	N	N-1	...	2	1		
A							
B							
C							
⋮							
Unused							
N	VxN	V(N-1)	...	Vx2	V	VΣN	$\dfrac{100 \times (N+1)}{2}$

The final score card

APPENDIX 3

A Preferendum Analysis

The following two examples, both rather hypothetical perhaps, show what might happen in the preferendum analyses of two contentious debates or elections. We will first have a look at a little five-option/candidate ballot, and then at a more complicated ten-option/candidate vote.

For the sake of simplicity, let us assume that 100 people have completed a full ballot, each casting his/her preference points as he or she might wish for all the options/candidates listed. Let us also assume that, as it so happens, 55 individuals gave 5 points to A, 10 gave 5 points to B, 20 gave 3 points to D, etc., and that the entire picture of how everybody voted looks like this:

OPTION OR	THE	VOTES				
CANDIDATE	5pts	4pts	3pts	2pts	1pt	Unused
A	55				45	
B	10	20	40	20	10	
C	20	20	20	20	20	
D		10	20	50	20	
E	15	50	20	10	5	
Unused						

So if we now press that second button to get the points totals, we will get the following display:

OPTION OR CANDIDATE	THE POINTS					TOTALS	LEVELS OF CONSENSUS
	5pts	4pts	3pts	2pts	1pt		
A	275				45	320	64%
B	50	80	120	40	10	300	60%
C	100	80	60	40	20	300	60%
D		40	60	100	20	220	44%
E	75	200	60	20	5	360	72%

Well even a cursory glance at the votes display would suggest that option/candidate A is seen to be very divisive and aconsensual; B and C are viewed with little enthusiasm; D is regarded as a very poor suggestion; but E enjoys some consensual support, it seems, and sure enough, E gets the highest score: 72%.

If the preferendum concerns a policy issue, the consensors will now form up a composite result based on option E, enriched if possible by any commensurate aspects of option A, perhaps by B and C though that's unlikely, and perhaps again by the negation of D.

If on the other hand it's an election of, say, two persons, then E and A will be the chosen two; and if of three persons, E, A and C - for although B ties with C, the latter gets more 5s - please see page 42.

For our second example, we'll take a ten-option vote. The panel displays are therefore a little more complex, but the logic is exactly the same. First the votes, and then the points:

OPTION or CANDIDATE	THE VOTES										
	10pts	9pts	8pts	7pts	6pts	5pts	4pts	3pts	2pts	1pt	Unused
A	30	20	10					5	15	20	
B	20	15	5					10	20	30	
C	20	10	10	5	5	5	5	10	10	20	
D	20	15	15	10	10	5		5	10	10	
E	10	10	10	10	10	10	10	10	10	10	
F		30	20	20	10	10	10				
G			20	40	30	10					
H			10	15	25	25	15	10			
I				10	10	20	25	25	10		
J						25	40	25	10		
Unused											

OPTION or CANDIDATE	THE POINTS										TOT	LEVELS OF CONS.
	10pts	9pts	8pts	7pts	6pts	5pts	4pts	3pts	2pts	1pt		
A	300	180	80					15	30	20	625	62.5% ·
B	200	135	40					30	40	30	475	47.5%
C	200	90	80	35	30	25	20	30	20	20	550	55.0%
D	200	135	120	70	60	25		15	20	10	655	65.5%
E	100	90	80	70	60	50	40	30	20	10	550	55.0%
F		270	160	140	60	50	40				720	72.0%
G			160	280	180	50					670	67.0%
H			80	105	150	125	60	30			550	55.0%
I				60	50	80	75	50	10		325	32.5%
J						125	160	75	20		380	38.0%

On a close inspection of the votes, we see that options/candidates A and B are both regarded as being very extreme; C is felt to be less extreme perhaps, but still rather divisive; and D, though slightly more popular, is still somewhat aconsensual. E, meanwhile, seems bland indeed. H, if we may jump a little, appears a bit empty, while I and J are viewed with scepticism if not scorn. But now, returning to F, we see that though it gets no 10s at all, it nevertheless gets a very good score; and even G, with no 9s or 10s to its name, is also seen as a good compromise.

Now there are some who say consensus politics will lead to weak decisions and mediocre candidates, what they often call the wet compromise. But, as we see here, that is not the case, for the run-of-the-mill will only get about 55%. Whereas a consensus, to be accepted, must go for 75%.

We may note in passing that C, E and H all get an exact mean level of consensus. The reason is simple, for all three received symmetrical voting patterns, so no wonder their totals are average. This would be even more apparent if we drew the relevant histograms.

Again, the consensors must interpret these results. Any policy decision will be a composite based on F as enhanced by G definitely, and D perhaps, etc.. While any election of, say, three representatives will see F, G and D elected, in that order.

When, as in this example, option F is indeed to be combined with option G, (that or candidates F and G are both declared elected), with levels of consensus L_f and L_g respectively, the new overall level of consensus, L_{fg}, may best be determined by the following formula:

$$L_{fg} = L_f + (100 - L_f)\% \times L_g$$

If, furthermore, option D is also incorporated (or if candidate D also gets elected), then this new overall level, L_{fgd}, shall be given by:

$$L_{fgd} = L_{fg} + (100 - L_{fg})\% \times L_d$$

And if only a third of option D is compatible with the FG amalgam, the answer will be:

$$L_{fgd} = L_{fg} + \frac{(100 - L_{fg})\% \times L_d}{3}$$

It must be stressed, however, that the above formulae can only be our best estimates because, as we saw on page 28, any one level of consensus can often be represented by quite a few histograms.

APPENDIX 4

Partial and Valid Votes

In any vote of N options/candidates, he who casts preference points for only 'n' of them will exercise only:

n + (n-1) + ... + 2 + 1 points.

In other words, in say a 10-option/candidate preferendum (or matrix vote), those who award (no matter how many) points to only one option/candidate will, in effect, exercise only 1 point on behalf of that option/candidate.

Those who vote for 2 options/candidates will exercise	$2 + 1 =$	3 points.
Those who vote for 3 will exercise	$3 + 2 + 1 =$	6 points.
Those who vote for 4	$4 + 3 + 2 + 1 =$	10 points.
Those for 5	$5 + 4 + 3 + 2 + 1 =$	15 points.
Those for 6	$6 + 5 + 4 + 3 + 2 + 1 =$	21 points.
for 7	$7 + 6 + 5 + 4 + 3 + 2 + 1 =$	28 points.
for 8	$8 + 7 + 6 + 5 + 4 + 3 + 2 + 1 =$	36 points.
for 9	$9 + 8 + 7 + 6 + 5 + 4 + 3 + 2 + 1 =$	45 points.
And only those who vote for all 10 options/candidates will exercise full		
	$10 + 9 + 8 + 7 + 6 + 5 + 4 + 3 + 2 + 1 =$	55 points.

So while the right hand column increases in mathematical progression, the left hand number - the number of points given to the voter's first choice - increases only in linear fashion. And that which might at first sight have seemed a little unfair - please see page 17 - is in fact (mathematical and therefore) logical enough.

To return to that earlier example where dad got only 1 point yet his daughter fair full 55, (pages 16-17), we should remember that there is a huge difference, mathematically speaking, between a score of:

10 + 0 + 0 + 0 + 0 + 0 + 0 + 0 + 0 + 0

and a score of:

1 + 0 + 0 + 0 + 0 + 0 + 0 + 0 + 0 + 0

at least in their effects on the final ten totals.

But there would be no difference - again, in this relative, mathematical regard - between a score of:

10 + 9 + 9 + 9 + 9 + 9 + 9 + 9 + 9 + 9

and a score of:

1 + 0 + 0 + 0 + 0 + 0 + 0 + 0 + 0 + 0 .

The important factor is not so much the total number of points each voter casts - 1, 55 or 10 + 9x9 - but rather, I emphasise, the relative effect:

As a result of dad's vote, by what margin has C increased its chances of success over the other options or candidates?

Accordingly, so far as dad's vote concerns the relative success of C and G, say, to take just two of the options, it matters not whether it is interpreted as

'C 10, G 9'

or

'C 1, G 0'.

There is an enormous difference, though, between dad's actual

'C 10, G 0',

and the way it must be counted,

'C 1, G 0'.

Partial votes

We will now take just a simple 6-option/candidate ballot, in which case the vote of he who gives 6 points to option/candidate C but nothing to anything/body else will be recorded as: 'C 1'.

If another writes 'C 6, E 5, A 4, F 3' and nothing else, her vote will be taken as:
'C 4, E 3, A 2, F 1'.

If a third votes somewhat haphazardly, giving 'C 6, E 5, F 1' and again nothing else, this will be recorded as:
'C 3, E 2, F 1'.

And lastly, if someone writes just 'C 6, E 3, F 1', this vote will also be recorded as:
'C 3, E 2, F 1'.

Valid votes

Moving on to possible invalid votes, let us just quote some further examples, again in a 6-option/candidate ballot.

If someone votes 'A 4, D 6, E 3 and F 5', it will be taken as a valid partial vote and read as follows:
'A 2, D 4, E 1, F 3'.

If another votes 'B 1, C 2, D 6, E 3 and F 5', this must also be taken as a valid partial vote. The voter may have wanted to say 'A 4', or she may have deliberately chosen 'A 0'. As the difference between the two is great, all the adjudicators can do is take what is clear, namely:
'B 1, C 2, D 5, E 3 and F 4'.

If yet a third votes 'A 4, B 1, C 3, D 6, E 3 and F 5', we may assume he has made just a small mistake and wished to give either C or E 3 points, and E or C 2 points. The others are not affected, so this vote may be taken as:
'A 4, B 1, C 2.5, D 6, E 2.5, F 5'.

Accordingly, if any voter wishes to bracket two or even three options/candidates together, this may duly be catered for. It is important to note, however, that the total number of effective points must not thus be altered.

So if someone votes 'A 4, B 1, C 2, D 6, E 3 and F 6', his vote will be recorded as 'A 4, B 1, C 2, D 5.5, E 3, F 5.5'.

And if someone else votes 'A 4, B 4, C 4, D 6, E 1 and F 5', it will be taken as 'A 3, B 3, C 3, D 6, E 1, F 5'.

On balance, however, it is better if those voting always make a deliberate preference. Certainly no-one should be allowed to bracket more than three options/candidates, lest old dad again, still madly in favour of C, once more rejects the spirit of consensus and votes:
'A 1, B 1, C 6, D 1, E 1, F 1'.
Although in theory and according to the above guidelines, his vote could be interpreted as:
'A 3, B 3, C 6, D 3, E 3, F 3',
this would still increase C's chances of relative success over all its rivals by a greater margin than would the votes of those who do not bracket their options/candidates. Such 'blanket-bracketing' must, therefore, be deemed invalid.

Overall, just as in PR-STV where those in charge of the count try to interpret any minor errors - subject to the approval of all the candidates - so too in consensus voting, small errors should be interpreted with some flexibility, subject to the consensors' directives and again, the candidates' approval.

APPENDIX 5

Maxima and Minima

The Preferendum

In all analyses, the consensors should be aware of the relevant theoretical levels which any one option or candidate might achieve.

The maximum possible level of consensus is always 100% of course, and while the theoretical minimum is zero, i.e., a total abstention on that particular option/candidate, the ideal minimum level of consensus is a whole load of 1s.

So when everyone votes for all options/candidates, the minima and average levels vary according to the following table:-

```
In a

3 - option/candidate poll the minimum level of consensus is  33%, the average  67%

4 - option/candidate poll the minimum level of consensus is  25%, the average  63%

5 - option/candidate poll the minimum level of consensus is  20%, the average  60%

6 - option/candidate poll the minimum level of consensus is  17%, the average  58%

7 - option/candidate poll the minimum level of consensus is  14%, the average  57%

8 - option/candidate poll the minimum level of consensus is  13%, the average  56%

9 - option/candidate poll the minimum level of consensus is  11%, the average  55%

10 - option/candidate poll the minimum level of consensus is  10%, the average  55%
```

or, just to keep the mathematician happy, the maximum, minimum and average levels of consensus are:

$$100\%, \quad \frac{100\%}{N} \quad \text{and} \quad \frac{100 \times (N+1)\%}{2N} \quad \text{respectively;}$$

where N is the number of options/candidates.

The average, by the way, does not denote a majority-vote-type threshold, all above enjoying a 'for', all below an 'against'. When voting on a shopping list of newspapers, to return to that earlier example, no one option excludes another, and the results of such a vote would indicate only which papers are very popular, and which less so, (although if no-one votes for 'The Sun', for example, further healthy conclusions may also be drawn).

A threshold exists if and when, in forming any subsequent composite, the consensors find that the more popular options already accepted mutually exclude the next most popular option.

The Modified Matrix and the Matrix Vote.

In these elections, the result is an entire sub-committee or a complete executive. If V is the valid vote in an election of X persons from a list of N candidates, then the maximum and minimum scores of any one candidate will be $(X \times V)$ and 0 respectively. Our main concern, however, relates to L, the level of consensus of the overall result, and this is given by the following formula:

$$L = \left\{ \frac{\text{total number of points cast for all winning candidates}}{\text{total number of points cast for all candidates}} \right\} \times 100\%$$

Thus the maximum level of consensus, 100%, would be achieved if all those voting only chose the successful ones.

APPENDIX 6

A Matrix Vote

Choose, in your own order of preference, six different persons from the approved list of candidates. Place the name of the candidate you most wish to see in government in the 6 points column opposite the post you want him/her to fill; place your next favourite in the 5 points column in another row of your choice; and so on.

* If you notate only one person for one post, you will exercise only 1 point for that person in that post.
* If you notate two persons, each for a different post, you will exercise 2 + 1 points respectively, a total of 3 points.
* If you notate three persons for three posts, you will exercise 3 + 2 + 1, a total of 6 points. And so on.
* And if you name six different persons for all 6 different posts, you will exercise full 6 + 5 + 4 + 3 + 2 + 1 = 21 points.

	Please enter your choice of names here below					
	6pts	5pts	4pts	3pts	2pts	1pt
Premier						
Deputy PM						
Min of Peace						
Min of Health						
Min of Tax						
Min of Land						

On completing a full ballot, there should be one name in each column, and one in each row, six different names in all.

APPENDIX 7

The Matrix Count.

In appendix 2, we were able to calculate the common consensus of just the three of us - thee, me and another - using a preferendum. Now, in similar style, using the ballot paper shown opposite, we will have a go at a matrix vote, so to find what is our common consensus on who should serve in a government of six from our parliament of ten, and the rules governing any partial votes shall be the same as those used in preferenda.

Having seriously considered all the candidates, let us say you decided to fill in your voting slip as follows:

	Your choice of names					
	6pts	5pts	4pts	3pts	2pts	1pt
Premier			Sam			
Deputy PM						Bob
Min of Peace	Jo					
Min of Health		Pat				
Min of Tax					Ann	
Min of Land				Tom		

Any casual observer could thus conclude you are absolutely committed to peace, and Jo, you feel, is the best one for that job. Health is also one of your priorities, while the post of deputy PM, in these days of consensus, is of little concern to you. In all, there is a lot of information to be gleaned from an examination of your completed ballot, but that's because you had a lot of choice.

You, of course, are different. I, old hack that I am, voted in a more traditional way:

	My choice of names					
	6pts	5pts	4pts	3pts	2pts	1pt
Premier	Fred					
Deputy PM		Bob				
Min of Peace					Sam	
Min of Health						Jo
Min of Tax				Ann		
Min of Land			Sean			

While another had this to say:

	Another's choice of names					
	6pts	5pts	4pts	3pts	2pts	1pt
Premier	Jo					
Deputy PM				Sam		
Min of Peace					Tom	
Min of Health		Pat				
Min of Tax			Mary			
Min of Land						Paul

If we now list all ten candidates and table the points received by each, we get the following display:

	Candidates										Relative Importance	Unused
	Jo	Fred	Pat	Bob	Sam	Sean	Mary	Tom	Ann	Paul		
Premier	6	6			4						16	
Deputy PM				5+1	3						9	
Min of Peace	6				2				2		10	
Min of Health	1		5+5								11	
Min of Tax							4	3+2			9	
Min of Land						4		3		1	8	
TOTALS	13	6	10	6	9	4	4	5	5	1	63	

By looking at the bottom row of individual totals, we can see who are our six most popular candidates: Jo, Pat, Sam, Fred, Bob, and either Tom or Ann. They shall form the government, so say the three of us. And because we three all used full 21 points, the final figure at the bottom right hand corner is $3 \times 21 = 63$; if it is not, the computer will be programmed to give another bleep.

Next, by examining the right hand column, we can see the degree of importance we attach to each post. The above matrix may thus be simplified as shown below, and please note the rearranged order of both candidates and ministerial posts:

	Candidates								Relative Importance
	Jo	Pat	Sam	Fred	Bob	Tom	Ann	Other	
Premier	(6)		4	6					16
Min of Health	1	(10)							11
Min of Peace	6		(2)		2				10
Deputy PM			3		(6)				9
Min of Tax						(5)	4		9
Min of Land						3		5	8
TOTALS	13	10	9	6	6	5	5	9	63

Now by looking at this matrix which, having deleted the 'other' column, we repeat here,

	Candidates							Relative
	Jo	Pat	Sam	Fred	Bob	Tom	Ann	Importance
Premier	(6)		4	6				16
Min of Health	1	(10)						11
Min of Peace	6		(2)			2		10
Deputy PM			3		(6)			9
Min of Tax							(5)	9
Min of Land						3		8
TOTALS	13	10	9	6	6	5	5	63

we can see in which ministerial post each successful candidate should serve. We simply take the highest individual scores some of which are shown bracketed, (10) and (6), for instance, and thus appoint the person concerned to the ministerial post indicated. In the event of a tie, priority is given first to the person with the higher total, and then to the more important post. In the above example, the consensors will thus reason according to the following logic:

The highest individual score is Pat's 10 for health, so she gets that job. Then, of the four 6s (shown in tint), the most popular person in the most popular post puts Jo in the premiership, and that rules out her second 6 for the peace post, as well as Fred's 6 for the premiership. Bob's 6 for deputy still stands, however. Next comes Ann's 5 for tax which puts paid to Tom's ambitions; (never mind, he was obviously one of the less popular figures in parliament, and he was only contending a minor post; all the tensions of a majoritarian vote play a much reduced part in any consensual contest). Finally, to allocate the last two, Sam with a 2 goes to peace, so Fred with a nothing goes to land.

Thus may we now draw up the following matrix, the result of all our deliberations, our tripartite consensus. (And even if three hundred of us had voted, the final picture would be just about as simple.)

	Successful Candidates						Relative
	Jo	Pat	Sam	Fred	Bob	Ann	Importance
Premier	6						16
Min of Health		10					11
Min of Peace			2				10
Deputy PM				6			9
Min of Tax						5	9
Min of Land					0		8
TOTALS	13	10	9	6	6	5	63

The final score card

Of all the 63 points cast, 49 of them were used to get the six successful candidates elected; this corresponds to a level of consensus of 77%.

Secondly, if we add up the above individual scores in the matrix, 29, we may ascertain how many of the points actually served their immediate intended purpose.

Thirdly, the numbers in the little squares within the matrix will be equal to or less than the totals shown in the bottom row. The greater the similarity, the more cohesive the result.

And lastly, we must be able to attach some significance to the straightness of the final diagonal, but I'll leave that to a more qualified mathematician to sort out.

We could, if you like, do another analysis. For of the 49 points cast in favour of the chosen six, 18 were yours, 17 mine and 14 another's. What's more, of the successful 29 points in the individual matrix scores, 8 were yours, 10 mine and 10 another's. Each, then, gets roughly a third, and if you lose a little on the consensual swing, you'll gain a *soupçon* on the roundabouts.

Generally speaking, therefore, it is fair to say that the matrix vote is highly proportional, and maybe more so than any other system of humble human origins.

In political fora, the person elected to a particular post will usually accept his/her selection. While in the smaller committees we mentioned on page 46, there may be those who, even if chosen by the consensus of all, prefer nevertheless to decline. This they can of course do, (just as at some future date they may choose to resign), in which case the post should go to the next most suited, while the one who declines should thereby lose the chance of competing for any other post, until any subsequent election.

If the list of candidates and posts has been drawn up correctly, however, such chopping and changing after the election should never be necessary.

APPENDIX 8

Freedom of Choice versus Abuse of Power

As a general principle of democracy, it is always better to cater for the maximum possible freedom of choice. For just as, yesterday, any increase of parliamentary power worked to reduce the power of the monarch, so too, to-day, any additional choice acquired by our representatives will serve to reduce the power of the party leaders. There can be little to fear in that.

Leaders, or those who aspire to be such, will be with us for a long time yet, I suppose. We must therefore ensure that the chances of these people ever becoming a *Stalin* or a Hitler are very much reduced, (and it is sobering to recall that while the first emerged in a one-party state, the second succeeded from within a supposed multi-party system).

As I have tried to demonstrate, consensus voting can be just such a guarantee. I should add, however, that the odds which follow are maxima, a) because political choices are never random,[67] and b) because these odds take no account of what happens if the aspiring despot tries to bribe, threaten or whip (to use the term still in British/Irish parliamentary parlance) the elected representatives to vote, not as they might wish to, but as he or she dictates.

The 'free vote' in Westminster is a rare occurrence. It is used at the discretion of the whips, it infers the members may at last vote according to their consciences, but on such emotive issues as capital punishment, many then prove they haven't even got one!

In consensus politics, every vote shall be free. And even if some politicians are cajoled against their better judgement, the odds will still be pretty long, because (almost) every vote shall be multi-optional.

In the sections which follow, we will look at the choice each consensus voting system offers its participants or, to put it another way, the much reduced chances of any leader to dominate.

The Preferendum

(In a 2-option/candidate referendum, there is a choice of only 2 possible opinions, and that is that.) In preferenda, though, it's like this:

In a

3 - option/candidate poll, there's a choice of	6	possible opinions and/or emphases,
4 - option/candidate poll, there's a choice of	24	possible opinions and/or emphases,
5 - option/candidate poll, there's a choice of	120	possible opinions and/or emphases,
6 - option/candidate poll, there's a choice of	720	possible opinions and/or emphases,
7 - option/candidate poll, there's a choice of	5,040	possible opinions and/or emphases,
8 - option/candidate poll, there's a choice of	40,320	possible opinions and/or emphases,
9 - option/candidate poll, there's a choice of	362,880	possible opinions and/or emphases;
and in a		
10 -option/candidate poll, there's a choice of	3,628,800	possible opinions and/or emphases.

or, as the mathematician would say, in an N-option preferendum, the total number of full opinions and/or emphases which may be expressed is:

N x (N-1) x (N-2) x ... x 2 x 1.

This is known as factorial N, and written as N!

Thus, in a simple N-option preferendum in which our parliamentarians are aiming to choose just the one simple policy, the theoretical chances of any such leader being able to dictate proceedings will be at least 1 in N; in practice, especially when compositing is involved, his/her chances are likely to be even more reduced.

Similarly, if we the electors or they the elected are electing a fixed number of persons, (X), from a choice of N candidates, or maybe our representatives are selecting X items from a "shopping list" of N possibles, each (and let's say she's a she) may choose any one of N persons or items as her first choice, any one of (N-1) as her second choice, and so on, and this she does X times.   In other words, she will have a choice of:

$$N \times (N\text{-}1) \times (N\text{-}2) \times \dots \times [N\text{-}(X\text{-}1)] \quad = \quad \frac{N!}{(N\text{-}X)!}$$

different ways of voting.   If the order in which these X persons or items are elected is of no particular importance - and there are of course X! different orders of preference in which X objects can be selected - then the probability of any one particular set of X being chosen will be:

$$1 \text{ in } \quad \frac{N!}{X! \times (N\text{-}X)!} \quad \text{where } N > X, \text{ and } X > 1$$

(formula A)

If, however, the order of elections does matter, the probability of any one particular order will be:

$$1 \text{ in } \quad \frac{N!}{(N\text{-}X)!}$$

(formula B)

If we refer to the example given on page 54, namely, a preferendum election for two representatives from a list of six, those concerned will have a choice of 720 different ways of voting, and the chances of any one party leader or whoever being able to insist on only his own proposals will be:

$$1 \quad \text{in} \quad \frac{6!}{2! \times (6-2)!}$$

$$= \quad 1 \quad \text{in} \quad \frac{6!}{2! \times 4!}$$

$$= \quad 1 \quad \text{in} \quad \frac{6 \times 5}{2}$$

$$= \quad 1 \quad \text{in} \quad 15.$$

If, however, he is saying that old so-and-so must be the chair, and whatshisname the deputy, his chances will be found by using formula B:

$$1 \quad \text{in} \quad \frac{6!}{(6-2)!}$$

$$= \quad 1 \quad \text{in} \quad \frac{6!}{4!}$$

$$= \quad 1 \quad \text{in} \quad 6 \times 5$$

$$= \quad 1 \quad \text{in} \quad 30.$$

The Modified Matrix

If they now choose a sub-committee of X persons from a ballot paper of N candidates, and if, again, it matters not in which order they are elected, an ambitious leader's chances of getting his own nominees chosen will be as above in the preferendum:

$$1 \text{ in } \frac{N!}{X! \times (N-X)!}$$

(formula A)

When the order of election does matter, the odds get tighter. If the old tyrant wants to insist on a certain number (Y) of named office bearers within this sub-committee, (where X > Y), then the likelihood of his total success will be:

$$1 \text{ in } \frac{N!}{(X-Y)! \times (N-X)!}$$

(formula C)

And if he's really intransigent and seeks to nominate not just Y but all X persons, and in his own particular order, his chances will be smaller still:

$$1 \text{ in } \frac{N!}{(N-X)!}$$

(formula B)

In the particular modified matrix of ten candidates mentioned on page 54, the chances of the despot getting his own chosen six may be ascertained using formula A:

$$1 \quad \text{in} \quad \frac{10!}{6! \times (10\text{-}6)!}$$

$$= \quad 1 \quad \text{in} \quad \frac{10 \times 9 \times 8 \times 7}{4 \times 3 \times 2}$$

$$= \quad 1 \quad \text{in} \quad 210.$$

Similarly, his chances of getting not only his four ordinary members (in any order of election), but his two named office bearers as well, will be found as per formula C:

$$1 \quad \text{in} \quad \frac{10!}{(6\text{-}2)! \times (10\text{-}6)!}$$

$$= \quad 1 \quad \text{in} \quad \frac{10!}{4! \times 4!}$$

$$= \quad 1 \quad \text{in} \quad \frac{10 \times 9 \times 8 \times 7 \times 6 \times 5}{4 \times 3 \times 2}$$

$$= \quad 1 \quad \text{in} \quad 6,300$$

Lastly, his chances of getting all his own six members elected in his own particular order will be given in accordance with formula B:

$$1 \quad \text{in} \quad \frac{10!}{4!}$$

=   1   in $10 \times 9 \times 8 \times 7 \times 6 \times 5$

=   1   in   151,200.

The Matrix Vote

If our elected representatives are now to elect an executive of X members from a list of N candidates using a matrix vote, the choice involved will be very large indeed.

Each - this one's a he - may choose any one of N candidates for any one of X posts, so his first choice is one of (NxX). For his second selection, he has a choice of (N-1) candidates for any one of (X-1) posts, that is, any one of $\{(N-1) \times (X-1)\}$ possibilities. And so on, X times. In theory, then, the total number of different ways of voting is:

$$\frac{N! \times X!}{(N-X)!} \quad \text{where again, } N > X.$$

(formula D)

So the chances of any abuse may be absolutely infinitesimal. Let us take the example shown in appendix 7, an executive of six ministers chosen from a list of ten candidates. In such a matrix vote, the total number of different ways of voting will be given by this formula D:

$$\frac{10! \times 6!}{(10-6)!}$$

$$= \quad \frac{10! \times 6!}{4!}$$

$$= \qquad 10! \times 6 \times 5$$

$$= \quad 10 \times 9 \times 8 \times 7 \times 6 \times 5 \times 4 \times 3 \times 2 \times 6 \times 5$$

$$\cong \qquad 100, 000,000$$

And that is just a simple example! If we now take the Irish *Dáil* and if all 166 TDs were to elect a government of 15 ministers in a matrix vote, each would be able to choose any one of those 166 members to serve in any one of these 15 ministerial posts, then any one of 165 to serve in any one of 14, and so on. In all, every TD would be able to vote in any one of 1.4×10^{45} different ways, give or take a squared million or so.

In the larger House of Commons where 651 MPs currently enjoy a cabinet of 22, each would have a choice of 6.2×10^{82} voting patterns.

It is all a great advance on 2.

APPENDIX 9

Voting Systems - a Critique

To be fair to the preferendum, criticism should be made of other voting-cum-electoral systems too. Well, even in 1918, it was *"claimed that there were over 300 alternative electoral systems in existence"*,[68] and there were probably quite a few voting procedures as well. To which I confess I have added two more. Now we are not going to discuss them all, not in this little volume anyway! So we'll confine our comments to those we have concentrated on in the text, though this time, we will start with an electoral system:

A Majority Voting in elections	E Majority Voting in debate
B AV	F Condorcet and the Preferendum
C PR-STV	G the Preferendum itself, and
D Condorcet	H Quota Preference Score

A - MAJORITY VOTING IN ELECTIONS

In the British first-past-the-post system, as inferred earlier, a winner needs the support of only the largest minority. Thus to take a practical example, the UK October 1974 general election result in Inverness was as follows:

Party	% share of the vote
Liberal	32.4%
SNP	29.6%
Conservative	22.0%
Labour	15.6%
Independent	0.4%

So 67.6% did not vote for the winner! Indeed, in Scotland as a whole on that occasion, 56 of the 71 MPs were elected on a minority vote.[69]

In certain situations, the consequences of such a system can be absolutely tragic: "...*only 48% of the Serbian electorate voted for the Socialist Party. Miloshevich had anticipated this eventuality by taking a leaf out of the British electoral book and designing a system whereby he would still enjoy absolute political control with less than 50% of the vote*".[70]

B - THE ALTERNATIVE VOTE

The main defect of AV has already been identified when, on contemplating Scotland's future in chapter 3, we saw how a tiny minority of floating voters could easily produce a quite different result. As a consequence, many an AV multi-option poll tends to deteriorate a little into what is just a variation on the majoritarian "two horse" race, so few go beyond three options.[71]

AV elections, however, can and do go beyond three candidates; they are, as we said, a great improvement on the majority vote, they help to ensure the extremist does not too easily succeed, and they are used by the Australians for their Lower House elections.[72]

C - PR-STV

The same arbitrariness may also be true of PR-STV, as shown by the following example taken from Dummett's *"Voting Procedures"*.[73]

Consider, then, an election with eight candidates A to G competing for four places, with a valid vote of 1000 and so a quota of 201. Totals of candidates achieving the quota are shown underlined, while those of the unsuccessful being eliminated are shown in brackets.

	1st stage		2nd stage		3rd stage		4th stage		5th stage		6th stage		7th stage	
A	204		-	-	-	-	-	-	-	-	-	-	-	-
B	190		3	193	47	240	-	-	-	-	-	-	-	-
C	120		0	120	48	168	39	207	-	-	-	-	-	-
D	95		0	(95)	-	-	-	-	-	-	-	-	-	-
E	98		0	98	0	98	0	98	0	98	2	(100)	-	-
F	100		0	100	0	100	0	100	0	100	48	148	44	192
G	96		0	96	0	96	0	96	6	102	47	149	56	205
H	97		0	97	0	97	0	97	0	(97)	-	-	-	-

The result is the election of A, B, C and G, in that order. Now consider exactly the same election, with exactly the same voting patterns except for the votes of ten individuals who previously cast their 1st preferences for A but who now give them to D. The count is as follows:

	1st stage		2nd stage		3rd stage		4th stage		5th stage		6th stage		7th stage	
A	194		0	194	0	194	3	197	2	199	1	200	1	201
B	190		0	190	0	190	2	192	2	194	2	196	1	197
C	120		0	(120)	-	-	-	-	-	-	-	-	-	-
D	105		24	129	80	209	-	-	-	-	-	-	-	-
E	98		24	122	30	152	1	153	70	223	-	-	-	-
F	100		23	123	0	123	1	(124)	-	-	-	-	-	-
G	(96)		-	-	-	-	-	-	-	-	-	-	-	-
H	97		25	123	10	133	1	134	50	184	19	203	-	-

The result is quite different: the election of D, E, H and then A. In a word, as Dummett clearly shows, PR-STV can be quite random in its results. The mathematical reason is obvious, for while in the upper table, for example, all of F's second preferences counted for nothing, in the lower diagram they were transferred with effect.

One of the many advantages of PR-STV over most other electoral systems in use is nevertheless overwhelming: it ensures almost full freedom of choice for the voter, and as we said earlier, the representation, not only of the majority, but also of any sizeable minority. In a four-seater constituency, for example, any minority of 25% or more is sure to be able to get someone elected.

What PR-STV does not do, however, and this is its greatest weakness, is to give any credence at all to the likes of *Ante Markovich* (please see page xi), the candidate who is perhaps the second preference of everybody, but the first of none.

D - CONDORCET

In that Scottish example of a 3-option ballot, we assumed most who favoured either independence I or the *status quo* S would opt for devolution D as a second choice, (please see page 13), and the Condorcet system worked well. But let us now consider a different example: the re-naming of Russia's second largest city. It should have been a poll based on a 3-option vote, with Leningrad, Petrograd and St. Petersberg all on the list, a poll in which the voters' orders of preferences would have been less predictable.

For the sake of simplicity, we will again assume a small electorate, this time of but five persons, voting like this:

	Pyotr	Petrov	Petrovna	Petrovich	Petinka
1st choice	StP	StP	P	L	L
2nd choice	P	P	L	P	StP
3rd choice	L	L	StP	StP	P

Taking Condorcet pairs as we did on page 15, we find that:

	StP > P	by	3:2
	P > L	by	3:2
and	L > StP	by	3:2

which leads to an extraordinary conclusion:

$$StP > P > L > StP$$

and we go round and round in circles, forever! Such a result which Condorcet himself recognised is called a cyclical majority or the paradox of voting, and in theory it can occur on numerous occasions. In the *Realpolitik* of nations, however, just as in our Scottish ballot, such a result would probably be less likely, unless the number of options is greater than 3, when all sorts of circles are possible.

E - MAJORITY VOTING IN DEBATE

If there are more than two options, and if it is decided that any winner must have at least 50% of the vote, chaos ensues. For to get such a result, there has to be a sort of knock-out competition. In the above Russian example, there could be a first round contest of StP v P, say, and the winner of that would then face L in the final. Doubtless that would suit all the L supporters very nicely. Indeed, if a little unscrupulous, they could vote for what they regard as the worse of the two in the first round, so to facilitate an easy victory for themselves in the second. But by then, the losers in the first round might also wish for what they now consider to be the worse.

So in fact, the results of such procedures tend to depend more on the luck of the draw and tactical voting, and rather less on the real or sincere wishes of the voters. To put it in a nutshell, pluralism and majoritarianism are mutually incompatible.

Even in the most simple of democratic scenarios, the same confusion is likely. For when a group of people debate first an amendment to a motion, and then the motion itself, there are again three possible outcomes:

A	the motion, as presented
B	the motion, amended
C	neither.

If the matter is very controversial, maybe some of the A supporters will think "better B than C," while others might feel "either A or C, but B never!" So too for B and C. In which case, in the first for-or-against vote on the amendment, (or the first round of what is in effect another knock-out competition), do C supporters vote for A or for B, an issue about which they obviously care less?

Yet if neither A nor B has an outright majority, the "log-rollers" of C may well be the decisive factor.[74] Our earlier suspicions, when we suggested many majority votes are decided by those who understand least of the issue in question, are confirmed. (Please see page 14.)

It is not just the people who are wrong; it is the system itself and the use of the 2-option vote which prompt such truly schizophrenic behaviour. And the fact that majority rule does not work whenever there are more than 2 options means that majority voting cannot, or at least should not, be part of any "peace process". The latter, by oft-repeated slogan if not indeed by definition, must allow any and every proposal to be *"on the table"*. So peace and majoritarianism are also mutually incompatible.

Even within the party system of politics and in the very institutions which believe in it, majority rule is a contradiction in terms. For if the majority itself makes its own decisions by majority vote, the ruling clique may only be a majority of the majority, the Thatcherite wing of the Tories, the Haughey faction of Fianna Fail, the Clinton 'half' of the Democrats or, to mention an extreme example, the Bolsheviks of the Social Democratic Workers' Party, and then the Stalinists of the Bolsheviks.

In theory at any rate, the clique need only be 51% of 51%, i.e., a mere 26% minority of the total. In practice, it may be 51% of even less! In that same Oct '74 UK general election, for example, Labour got 39% of the vote (and half the seats in the House); in '79, the Tories got 44% (and 53% of parliament). Well, 51% of 39% is only 19.9%, of 44% just 22.4%! No wonder Lord Hailsham derided the English system as an *"elective dictatorship"*.[75]

Finally, we should mention yet one more reason why, within any society, majority voting does not work at all well.

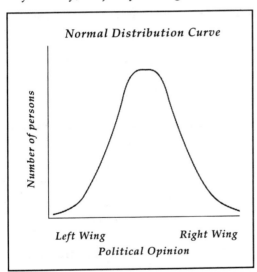

Normal Distribution Curve

Number of persons

Left Wing   *Right Wing*
Political Opinion

Like any other variable common to our species, many social opinions tend to fall on a so-called normal distribution curve. If, then, as in so many 2-option votes, the issue is divisive, the result will probably be decided by the middle, namely, the floating voters at or near the peak of the curve, those from a relatively small spectrum of opinion. But because the two options on the voting paper do not in all probability represent this part of the spectrum, many of these folk will not bother to vote at all. They are, indeed, the silent majority, and maybe, who knows, the real greater number!

F - CONDORCET AND THE PREFERENDUM

In the above Condorcet example of a cyclical majority, (page 113), it is interesting to note that a preferendum count would also give an exact tie:

	VOTES			POINTS			TOTALS	LEVELS OF CONSENSUS
	3pts	2pts	1pt	3pts	2pts	1pt		
StP	2	1	2	6	2	2	10	67%
P	1	3	1	3	6	1	10	67%
L	2	1	2	6	2	2	10	67%

There again, as no option gains the required level of 75%, such a result would not qualify in any case. In other instances of a cyclical majority, the preferendum scores would still give an indication, if not indeed a result.

Consider, please, a slightly different Russian electorate:

Pyotr	Petrov	Pavlov	Petrovna	Pavlova	Pavlovich	Petinka
StP	StP	StP	P	P	L	L
P	P	L	L	L	StP	StP
L	L	P	StP	StP	P	P

The Condorcet scores are now:

$$StP > P \quad by \quad 5:2$$
$$P > L \quad by \quad 4:3$$
$$and \quad L > StP \quad by \quad 4:3$$

which again means that:

$$StP > P > L > StP$$

but this time the preferendum scores would be:

	VOTES			POINTS			TOTALS	LEVELS OF CONSENSUS
	3pts	2pts	1pt	3pts	2pts	1pt		
StP	3	2	2	9	4	2	15	71%
P	2	2	3	6	4	3	13	62%
L	2	3	2	6	6	2	14	67%

Admittedly, this does not produce an answer with a score of 75%+. But as we know, the preferendum procedure can cope with such an outcome. The purpose here is only to show that where Condorcet may fail, the preferendum does not.

And vice versa? When Condorcet works, does the preferendum sometimes fail? Well Condorcet laid down a criterion which demands that the eventual winner must always be favoured by a majority. This the preferendum will not always comply with, in theory. In practice, however, given the facts that:

a) when electing candidates, at least two shall always be successful; and

b) when selecting policies, unless the winning option gets a very high score (in which case, doubtless it does comply), then at least two options will be formed into a composite;

then in all probability, it will always comply, and more!

But let us return to the theory, for even in those cases where the preferendum result does not meet the criterion, the winning option will undoubtedly be considered by (the majority of) that majority to be at least a good compromise option, for otherwise, how could it possibly have received such a high score?

And it is not the wish of a majority which must be the criterion of a true democracy, but rather, everybody's best compromise!

G - THE PREFERENDUM

There are two possible weaknesses of the preferendum I would like to discuss, and doubtless the first (which we mentioned on pages 37-39), is also applicable to the matrix vote:

a) the possible manipulation of the vote by a majority;

and

b) the apparent inevitability of a 75% level of consensus, whenever the consensors decide to form a composite.

a) Manipulation by a majority.

Let us first consider a forum of 100 persons, in which 51% are rabid protagonists of something, and 49% antagonists. In an election of, say, three persons, where all the candidates are either extremely pro or very anti, the majority could, in theory, act *en bloc* and vote as one; in which case, the minority might choose to retaliate by using exactly the same tactics. The worst possible result of a most bitter election would look like this:

	THE VOTES									
CANDIDATE	10pts	9pts	8pts	7pts	6pts	5pts	4pts	3pts	2pts	1pt
A pro	51									49
B pro		51							49	
C pro			51					49		
D pro				51			49			
E pro					51	49				
F pro					49	51				
G anti				49			51			
H anti			49				51			
I anti		49							51	
J anti	49									51

In which case, the points table would be as follows:

CANDIDATE	THE POINTS										TOT	LEVELS of CONSENSUS
	10pts	9pts	8pts	7pts	6pts	5pts	4pts	3pts	2pts	1pt		
A pro	510									49	559	55.9%
B pro		459							98		557	55.7%
C pro			408					147			555	55.5%
D pro				357			196				553	55.3%
E pro					306	245					551	55.1%
F pro					294	255					549	54.9%
G anti				343			204				547	54.7%
H anti			392					153			545	54.5%
I anti		441							102		543	54.3%
J anti	490									51	541	54.1%

and the result would be most unproportional - the election of A, B and C, three wretched pros, the most bigoted ones at that, and even if candidates D to G were nice moderates, it would not make an iota of difference. Furthermore, if such a result could be fixed by just a 51% majority, how much easier would it be for a larger, say 60%, monolith?

In many instances, I suspect, the results of a PR-STV election would be similar to those of a preferendum, especially if the voters make full use of their preferences. But in this example of a totally polarised society, a PR-STV election of three would give the following much fairer result: a quota of 26, the election of A and J, and then B by default:

	1st stage	2nd stage		3rd stage	
A pro	<u>51</u>	-	-	-	-
B pro	0	25	25	0	25
C pro	0	0	0	0	0
D pro	0	0	0	0	0
E pro	0	0	0	0	0
F pro	0	0	0	0	0
G anti	0	0	0	0	0
H anti	0	0	0	0	0
I anti	0	0	0	23	23
J anti	49	0	<u>49</u>	-	-

This weakness of the preferendum applies more to the election of persons, and less to the resolution of policy. For in the latter instance, if the consensors have done their job properly, the options listed would cover a broad enough spectrum, so only A and J, say, would be extreme, and given such a choice, total polarisation would be highly unlikely. Furthermore, when the "winning" levels of consensus are so low - 55.9% - the consensors would no doubt order a resumption of the debate.

Similarly, in the election of persons, if the consensors have ensured a fair balance, the theoretical disaster would never occur in practice. For if any party did try to dominate proceedings by loading the ballot paper, the result would be a two round contest as described on page 43, in which case such a group would soon find its comeuppance.

The weakness, then, concerns only the hypothetical, for in the world at large, such a homogenous majority would rarely if ever be found. As we pointed out on page 38, even Northern Ireland has never divided itself into two extreme camps, and the very existence of other parties and more especially of non-party folk suggests most societies could indeed afford to progress to the preferendum, if only because its deployment would help to prevent the emergence and/or survival of such blocs.

In Bosnia, too, though the bitter war continues, there are still those who refuse to take the side which others of their religion and/or descent demand. Believe it or not, it is these very people - the real Yugoslavs[76] - whom "the peace process" has disenfranchised. And the men of division, Boban and *Karadzhich*, fly to Geneva.

Because abuse in the preferendum will be far lower than that which is currently the norm in politics, perhaps its main weakness will lie in the fact that some will opt to boycott. Which is what happens under majority rule.[77] Again it must be stressed that the best way to obviate this risk is via the widespread adoption of consensual procedures in lands at peace.

b) Levels of consensus - 75%, more or less?

In theory, in any say 10-option preferendum, some options will get an above-average sum, a few rather mean totals, and the others scores somewhat below par. And, as we now know, either the result will produce one clearly preferred option, or there will be a close result between two or more popular options.

In the latter case, while a full composite of the first two might well produce a final level of consensus in excess of 75%, so too might an amalgam of the first and third options. So who is to say 75% consensus is sufficient, especially on those occasions when the second and third options are mutually exclusive.

Using the formulas advanced in appendix 5, any composite of options F and G will give a level of consensus L_{fg} as follows over the page:

$$L_{fg} = L_f + \frac{(100 - L_f)\% \times L_g}{x}$$

where x is the degree of compatibility of G with F.

Accordingly, when the first two options are only a little above average, with option F getting say 60% and option G 59% - (and this suggests the next most popular option will also be very close, option D, say, with 58%) - the resulting composite L_{fg} will enjoy, if, that is, the two are totally mutually compatible:

	60%	+	(100 - 60)% x 59%
=	60%	+	40% x 59%
=	60%	+	24%
=	84%		

while a similar composite of F and D would enjoy 83%. Close indeed. So can 75% really be an acceptable level of consensus, if different composites from the same results all get scores above that norm?

There again, if only a third of option G is compatible with F, the resulting composite would enjoy:

$$60\% + \frac{(100 - 60)\% \times 59\%}{3}$$

=	60%	+	8%
=	68%		

For the moment, at any rate, we are close to 75%.

Now as always, some may prefer to hand in only a partial vote. If a few do not vote for, say, option G, G's overall total will be correspondingly reduced, (as too a little that of option F), and so also the overall level of consensus of the composite.

If, to be specific, a valid vote of V persons participates in a preferendum of N options to only P%, where, it is proposed,

$$P \quad = \quad \frac{\Sigma n}{V \times N} \quad x \quad 100\%$$

with Σn being the sum of the number of options voted for by all those voting, then the overall level of consensus achieved by any composite of options F and G will be given by the following:

$$L_{fg} \quad = \quad L_f \quad + \quad \frac{(P - L_f)\% \times L_g}{x}$$

all of which tends to suggest that those who decide not to vote for option G will thereby reduce the overall level of consensus achieved by the winning combination. This makes the level of 75% sound just about right, but it also emphasises the fact that consensus voting is very much a collective act, and an acceptable result is utterly dependant on all who vote! If overall participation is low, nothing will get the required 75%, so all will have to go back to those round table discussions in a search for yet more possible compromise options, and then another vote. It also means that not only those who want to win should turn out to vote, but so too should those who do not want to lose. Democracy is indeed for everybody!

In other words, the democratic process should never allow a few Yugoslav or Northern Ireland extremists to gain a victory via only their own supporters. And that was where we started this book, on page x.

Our task is complete. What we may now say with absolute certainty, is this: that on any controversial matter, 100% consensus will rarely be achieved, but the absence of such a high level of agreement amongst everybody should not be used as an excuse for resorting to a process which may allow everything to be decided by as few as 51% of those present!

As an absolute minimum, resort should first be given to consensus voting, with a goal of 75% level of consensus support, from everyone. And time will tell whether a slightly higher or lower figure would be more appropriate.

H - QUOTA PREFERENCE SCORE

QPS is an excellent example of the art of compromise, for it combines the good points of PR-STV with those of Preference Score or the Borda system, and thus eliminates the defects of both. A full description of the original version is given in Dummett's work,[57] and what follows here is an outline of an improved version, a mixture of PR-STV and the preferendum.

For such a combination to be effective, the partially completed ballot must be treated in exactly the same way in the PR-STV half of the count as it is in the preferendum. Accordingly, may I suggest that for the purposes of the former, a vote for only x of N candidates should have a value of x/N. Thus the vote of one who, in a 5-candidate contest, votes for only 3 of them, will have an STV value of 0.6

Consider, then, another small electorate of only 14 persons choosing just two representatives from a hypothetical field of five English prospective parliamentary candidates whom we shall identify as follows:

a left-wing Socialist	S_L
an erstwhile colleague from the right	S_R
a Liberal	L
a pink Tory	T_L
and	
a Thatcherite	T_R

Imagine that the 14 constituents vote as shown below:

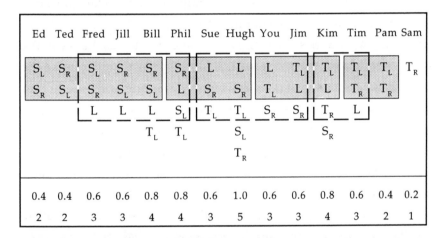

Ed	Ted	Fred	Jill	Bill	Phil	Sue	Hugh	You	Jim	Kim	Tim	Pam	Sam
S_L	S_R	S_L	S_R	S_R	S_R	L	L	L	T_L	T_L	T_L	T_L	T_R
S_R	S_L	S_R	S_L	S_L	L	S_R	S_R	T_L	L	L	T_R	T_R	
		L	L	L	S_L	T_L	T_L	S_R	S_R	T_R	L		
				T_L	T_L		S_L			S_R			
							T_R						
0.4	0.4	0.6	0.6	0.8	0.8	0.6	1.0	0.6	0.6	0.8	0.6	0.4	0.2
2	2	3	3	4	4	3	5	3	3	4	3	2	1

Of the above two lines of figures, the upper line is the STV value for each vote, while the lower line shows the number of preference points each voter casts for their favourite candidate in the preferendum.

Ed, for instance, votes for only two of the five candidates, S_L and S_R. He thus gives his favourite S_L a score of 0.4 in the STV count and 2 points in the preferendum, while to his second choice S_R he gives 1 preferendum point.

Jill, meanwhile, gives S_R 0.6 in the STV count, and she gives S_R, S_L and L 3, 2 and 1 points respectively in the preferendum.

The PR-STV count is:

$S_L = 1.0$ $S_R = 2.6$ $L = 2.2$ $T_L = 2.4$ $T_R = 0.2$

the preferendum scores are:

$S_L = 15$ $S_R = 25$ $L = 24$ $T_L = 20$ $T_R = 7$

and the total STV value of all 14 votes is 8.4 This we divide by the number of seats plus one, 2 + 1, to get 2.8, so then we can say the quota is 2.9. As none of the five candidates gets such a score, no-one gets elected at this stage.

We therefore move to the second stage and look for any possible pair of candidates with a combined STV score of 2.8 or more. There are four contenders shown above in the tinted boxes, but only the S_L/S_R team makes the grade with 2.8 exactly. We now examine the two members of that team, and choose the one with the higher preferendum score, in this case S_R with 25.

In the third stage, we look for any trio with a score of 2.8, and there are two, $S_L/S_R/L$ and $L/S_R/T_L$, shown here in the dotted-lined boxes. In both, L has the highest score, so L is the second candidate elected.

That's it - the two successful candidates are S_R and L. In other similar elections, if this stage is reached and still there are places to be filled, we simply take the next highest preferendum scores.

BIBLIOGRAPHY AND NOTES

Politics, conflict resolution, democracy, voting mechanisms, consensus, human psychology, the subject matter is enormous. But because the emphasis of this volume is on elections and decision-making, I have deliberately confined the following list of recommended works to those which concern voting and/or party politics. Other relevant works are mentioned in the notes.

From among the first group of books shown below, I would like to make especial mention of the volume by Professor Dummett.

The second set covers a more general politics, and while some of these books might refer to the inadequacies of the 2-option vote, they do not give a detailed criticism, let alone propose any remedy.

"Voting Procedures" by Michael Dummett.[19]
"Theory of Voting" by Robin Farguharson.[53]
"The Theory of Committees and Elections" by Duncan Black.[18]
"Social Choice and Individual Values" by Kenneth Arrow.[54]

"On Liberty" by John Stuart Mill.[37]
"The Social Contract" by Jean-Jacques Rousseau.[12]
"The Meaning of the Russian Revolution" by *Lev Tolstoy.*[33]
"Presidents above Party" by Ralph Ketcham.[21]
"The Party System" by Hilaire Belloc and Cecil Chesterton.[38]
"The People and the Party System" by Vernon Bogdanor.[47]

NOTES TO THE TEXT

1   *"The Collected Poems of John Hewitt"* edited by Frank Ormsby (Blackstaff Press, 1991) p 537.

2   Glenny, Misha, *"The Fall of Yugoslavia"* (Penguin, 1992) pp 147-8.

3   Thompson, Mark, *"A Paper House"* ([Hutchinson] Vintage, 1992) p 319.

4/5 From **The New Shorter Oxford English Dictionary**, (Clarendon Press) 1993.

6   **Steinberg**, Jules, *"Locke, Rousseau and the Idea of Consent"* (Greenwood Press, 1978) p 60, reprinted with permission of Greenwood Publishing Group, Inc., Westport, CT.

7   From the above dictionary,[4] future editions of which I hope will no longer describe 'consensus' as *"the majority view"*.

8   See **Buchanan**, James and **Tullock**, Gordon, *"The Calculus of Consent"* (University of Michigan, 1962), a book which first identifies some of the many disadvantages of majority voting, but then proceeds to praise one, this abuse of log-rolling, as if it negates some of the other wrongs.

9   Karl von Clausewitz: *"War is the continuation of politics by other means."*

10 **Van der Post**, Laurens, *"Jung and the Story of Our Time"* ([Chatto and Windus] Penguin, 1976). In fact, if we compare the individual human being to humanity in general, as Dietrich Bonhoeffer and others have done, then our habit of forever deciding so many questions on the basis of only two options could well be described as another *"symptom of* [our collective] *schizophrenia,"* p 268.

11 *Dostoyevsky, Fyodor Mikhailovich.* And while others later coined the term 'schizophrenia', perhaps it was *Dostoyevsky* who first identified the condition in one and/or two of his literary heroes, *Yakov Golyadkin* in *"The Double"*.

12 Terms used by Jean-Jacques **Rousseau** in his famous work *"The Social Contract"* (J M Dent, 1975).

13 *"A Multi-option Referendum - Let the People Decide"* (SNP, 1992) which, for reasons unstated, just "assumes" such a poll shall be conducted under AV, without even a mention of Condorcet or de Borda.

Notes to pages 14 - 15

14   The late Frank Maguire, the MP for Fermanagh S. Tyrone, was a
     republican perhaps but a publican definitely. Prior to that
     momentous vote, he had not frequented England let alone the House
     of Commons. Then, however, he chose to play a part. Without
     telling the many journalists of his voting intentions, he travelled to
     London, got to the House, found the right entrance, took his seat...
     and abstained, despite having been offered *"a drink or two [by the]
     Minister of State"* (**Belfast Telegraph** - 29.3.79). Callaghan's
     government fell by 1 vote.

15   If Jake changes his mind from DIS to DSI, the overall Condorcet
     result is: D > S by 7:4, D > I by 7:4 and S > I by 6:5, so D still wins.
     The result also stays the same with a preferendum:

	VOTES			POINTS			TOTALS	LEVELS OF
	3pts	2pts	1pt	3pts	2pts	1pt		CONSENSUS
S	4	2	5	12	4	5	21	64%
I	4	1	6	12	2	6	20	61%
D	3	8	-	9	16	-	25	76%

While if Jack persuades Jock to vote not SDI but IDS, the overall
Condorcet result is: D > S by 8:3, D > I by 6:5 and I > S by 7:4, so D
remains supreme, as too under a preferendum:

	VOTES			POINTS			TOTALS	LEVELS OF
	3pts	2pts	1pt	3pts	2pts	1pt		CONSENSUS
S	3	1	7	9	2	7	18	55%
I	5	2	4	15	4	4	23	70%
D	3	8	-	9	16	-	25	76%

Or if Jock persuades Jack, Condorcet gives: D > S by 6:5, D > I by 8:3
and S > I by 6:5 which still leaves D on top, as yet again in the
preferendum:

	VOTES			POINTS			TOTALS	LEVELS OF
	3pts	2pts	1pt	3pts	2pts	1pt		CONSENSUS
S	5	1	5	15	2	5	22	67%
I	3	2	6	9	4	6	19	56%
D	3	8	-	9	16	-	25	76%

The stability of the preferendum is, as it were, automatic. For the
common consensus is the calculated average, and the latter, as in
any such sum, cannot be too adversely affected by the vacillations,
manoeuvres or deliberate disruptions of only a small minority.

Notes to pages 20 - 57

16   Irish News, May 3rd 1977, in a letter to the editor.

17   If 75% give a certain option 10 points, and 25% give that same option their 1s, the level of consensual support for the implementation of that option will be:

$$\frac{75 \times 10 + 25 \times 1}{10} \quad = \quad \frac{750 + 25}{10} = \quad \frac{775}{10} \quad = \quad 77.5\%$$

18   **Black**, Duncan, *"The Theory of Committees and Elections"* (Cambridge, 1958) p 182.

19   **Dummett**, Michael, *"Voting Procedures"* (Oxford University [Clarendon] Press, 1984) p 179, a conclusion which a) relates only to questions of policy, and b) is based on all concerned submitting fully completed ballot papers. With partial voting, the preferendum is even more likely to give the *"finest outcome"*.

20   **Van der Post**, p 217.

21   **Ketcham**, Ralph, *"Presidents Above Party"* (University of North Carolina, 1984) quoting Henry Bolinbroke on p 60.

22   **Van der Post**, p 268.

23   From the **New Shorter Oxford English Dictionary** definition of candid, which rather suggests that in earlier times, candidates were not meant to promote themselves, but to be promoted by others.

24   And full acknowledgement should here be made to the one who first proposed the name 'preferendum', a Lancastrian called Pete whom I met among the European Greens in Dover in 1984. His second name, alas, I forget, but his first is nice.

25   **Dummett**, p 4.

26   The Borda system is similar in many respects to the preferendum. The main differences concern a) the treatment of partially-completed ballots; b) the acceptance of possible mutual inclusivity between some options; c) the subsequent formation of composite results; and d) the concept of levels of consensus.

27   **Baker**, Keith Michael, *"Condorcet - From Natural Philosophy to Social Mathematics"* (University of Chicago, 1975) quoting Jean d'Alembert on p 15.

28   **Ketcham**, quoting John Dryden's *"Absalom and Achitopel"* on p 21.

Notes to pages 57 - 59

29   **Baker** on Condorcet, p 229.

30   In theory, the mathematician might suggest, the rule by which points shall be awarded to the voters' various preferences could be directly proportional, arithmetic, logarithmic or whatever. In practice, the politician may argue, the punter should be allowed the choice, to give 10, 9, 8, 7... or 10, 10, 7, 7... or even 12, 8, 7, 7... if he/she so wishes.

As is only to be expected, different scoring schemes produce different results. So only one will do. And if the choice of points is left to the voter, the spirit of consensus will be lost. So only one can do.

We should therefore use in politics the same norms we use elsewhere, and in most spheres of life, we use a straight linear scale of whole integers. Whether by a nose, a head or a length, horses still come first and second. In school, we all got marks out of 10, some of us not very many, and I too failed my 11+. Earlier still on the nursery floor, with scant regard to both the quadratic and volumetric measure, most of us managed our first ever preferendum by putting lots of different boxes into order, carefully balancing one smaller on top of the other slightly bigger, (before then knocking them down). So throughout life, from first to last, we often use a 'linear language' of comparatives and superlatives.

The scoring used in the preferendum - a linear scale with a utility function (as it is called) of 1 between ordinals - is only a numerical equivalent of our everyday use of words.

31   **Ketcham**, quoting from George Washington's farewell address of 1796 on p 93.

32   **Rousseau**, Jean-Jacques, *"The Social Contract and Discourses"* (J M Dent, 1975) p 240.

33   *Tolstoy, Lev Nikolayevich*, writing in *"Russian Intellectual History: An Anthology"* (Columbia University, 1966) by Marc Raeff, p 329.

34   **Ketcham**, p 127.

35   Ibid, quoting Ralph Waldo Emerson on p 175.

36   **Lyons**, F S L, *"Ireland Since the Famine"* (Fontana, tenth impression, 1986) pp 474-5. It must be pointed out, however, that O'Higgins still believed in majority rule, at least in so far as the question of Irish independence was concerned. But perhaps, if he had lived...

Notes to pages 59 - 66

37   See House of Commons Debates of 30.5.1867, 3rd series, Vol 187, col 1351, when Mill gave an impassioned speech for PR-STV. Furthermore, in his famous essay *"On Liberty"*, he advised society *"to be on its guard against 'the tyranny of the majority'"*. And in an introduction to that essay, Richard Wollheim shows how Mill believed *"the government of the whole by a mere majority of the people is not democracy at all, but is often confused with it"*. *"Three Essays"* by John Stuart **Mill**, (Oxford University Press, 1975) pp 9 and xvii.

38   **Belloc,** Hilaire and **Chesterton,** Cecil, *"The Party System"* (Howard Latimer, 1913) p 19.

39   *Gorbachev, Mikhail Sergeyevich, "Perestroika"* (English edition, Collins, 1987) p 216. The conclusion is an intriguing one, namely, that the American democratic system is actually a form of one-party state!

40   My main contribution to the USSR's democratisation debate was published in **Moscow News** No 6/89, and it was interesting to observe, as did *Vitaly Tretyakov*, the deputy editor, how *Gorbachev* himself then started to use the word 'consensus' - see for example New York Times of 26.3.89

41   Only one year later, however, in his determination to be president, he was back to majority rule: *"Konsensusa nyet,"* he shouted, *"i ne budet!"* (*"There is no consensus, and there's not going to be any either!"*) - *Gorbachev*, live in Congress, March 1990.

42   Black, p 180.

43   Dummett, p 5. In the 1870's, Dodgson managed to publish just three papers on the subject, all of which are reprinted in the volume by Black.18

44   Black, in his introduction.

45   Dummett, p 4.

46   Ibid, in his epilogue.

47   **Bogdanor,** Vernon, *"The People and the Party System"* (Cambridge University Press, 1981). By another happy coincidence, STV also seems to have been invented at least twice, in England by a schoolmaster called Thomas Hill, and in Denmark by their then Minister of Finance, Carl Andrae. Its main protagonist, however, was a most un-Thatcherite nineteenth century Tory - Thomas Hare

Notes to pages 66 - 68

- who worked hard but in vain.

For in 1884, when the present British system was enacted, it was *"shaped throughout by the needs and interests of the party leaders, and settled, symbolically, in a private inter-party conclave"*. Ibid, p 113.

48   *"A Citizens' Inquiry - The Opsahl Report on Northern Ireland"* edited by Andy Pollak, (Lilliput, 1993) p 111. In an otherwise excellent report, the commissioners make just a few passing references to the preferendum, while the matrix vote, that which could be the very basis of a power-sharing arrangement far superior to that proposed in the Sunningdale Agreement, they do not even mention.

49   **McRae,** Kenneth D, *"Conflict and Compromise in Multilingual Societies - Switzerland"* (Waterloo: Wilfrid Laurier University Press, 1983) quoting Warner Kagi on p 105.

50/1   Ibid, pp 106 and 127.

52   **Dummett,** p 5.

53   **Buchanan** and **Tullock** certainly do this, but so too does Robin **Farquharson** in his much more scientific *"Theory of Voting"* (New Haven, 1969).

54   As in **Dummett's** scholarly work, (which I suspect only he would describe as containing *"nothing more formidable than a linear equation,"* p 295). And too in **Arrow,** Kenneth's *"Social Choice and Individual Values"* ([2nd edition] Yale University Press, 1963). *"In the theory of elections,"* he writes on p 12, *"alternatives are mutually exclusive."*

If the (political) question is asked correctly, however, then no matter what the debate, the subsequent vote should consist not of two mutually exclusive options, but rather of a range of options. In which case, inevitably, not all the options listed will be totally mutually exclusive of all the others! Their theories, fascinating stuff, are nevertheless somewhat divorced from reality.

Even candidates should not be seen in such a stark light. Was Bush really that different from another white, male, right-wing, 'American' nationalist, Clinton? Or for that matter, was *Trotsky* really the complete contrast to *Stalin?*

55   An example is **Deutsch,** Morton *"The Resolution of Conflict,"* (Yale University Press), 400 pages of almost irrelevant nonsense, with 'laboratory' games more suited to the kindergarten. Some more sensible advice is contained in **Fisher,** Roger and **Ury,** William's

Notes to pages 68 - 73

"Getting to Yes" and **Ury's** *"Getting Past No"*, but on a political level, even these could be described as rather naive.

56   **Shuster,** David, *"Teaming for Quality Improvement - A Process for Innovation and Consensus"* (Prentice Hall, 1990). Though they include what look like re-hashed versions of Condorcet and de Borda, his proposed voting systems are extremely long-winded and largely unsuited for any serious clash of interests, be it in the boardroom or the political chamber. Nice to see, though, that he also uses the term *"consensus voting"*.

57   Please see **Dummett,** pp 284-296.

58   **Black,** p 75, a reference which the author also applied to Condorcet. With both, however, he was talking of elections rather than votes on matters of policy. The logic of the preferendum suggests, of course, not only that extremists will fade, but so too will political parties!

59   **Belloc,** p 193.

60   One referendum was actually designed to be lost - the 1979 Scottish devolution poll. 51.6% of Scots voted in favour but, fearing such democracy (Rousseau again), the English parliament had earlier changed the rules to insist that the threshold of victory would be, not just 50% of the turnout, but 40% of the entire electorate!

61   Nearly all the Danish politicians wanted a 'yes', but in June 1992, only 49.3% of the people agreed. The former therefore added a few sweeteners, and in the second round one year later, 56.7% said yes.

62   The politicians (Fianna Fail) wanted majority voting, but the people who had elected them still wanted PR-STV. In the first 1959 referendum, 51.8% voted against any change. Undeterred by this demonstration of the people's will, the politicians tried again, in 1968, in a second referendum. But still the people said no, 61% this time! And it is sobering to recall that the reason why the democracy called Ireland has such a good voting system is not because the Dáil wanted it, but because the democrats in the British parliament imposed it! On foreigners, yes, but on themselves? Heavens, no! (Re the Irish divorce referendum, please see note 64.)

63   The anti-nuke lobby won the 1978 vote by 50.5% to 49.5%.

64   Such an emotive issue should never have been reduced to only two options. But in 1986, they did just that. The result was a most bitter campaign, and a victory for the 19th century by some 63%.

Notes to pages 73 - 121

65 McRae, p 131.

66 A quotation from Professor J L Synge used by Professor C A **Coulson** in his inaugural lecture of 28.10.52, *"The Spirit of Applied Mathematics"* (Oxford University Press, 1953). Reprinted by permission of Oxford University Press.

67 ...whereas the laws of mathematical probability assume all possibilities to be equally likely.

68/9 **Bogdanor,** pp 209 and 211.

70 **Glenny,** p 41. *Miloshevich* got just 52% of the vote, i.e., 25% of the electorate. But because of his system, he nevertheless gained 78% of the seats in parliament.

71 There have in fact been eleven multi-option referenda so far this century, including one in Guam where there were six options on the ballot paper! One such 3-option vote was the 1980 Swedish nuclear power referendum, which they nevertheless decided to operate as a straight majority vote! So while one of the options was definitely 'against', both the other two counted as 'for'. (Information Section, Embassy of Sweden.)

72 **Bogdanor,** p 169.

73 **Dummett,** pp 280-1.

74 For a more detailed criticism, see **Farquharson's** superb book.[53]

75 1976 Dimbleby lecture, (BBC) It is not just majority voting which has led the sovereignty of parliament to be hijacked by the government to thus become the sovereignty of cabinet, a state of affairs which Hailsham rightly bemoans. His solution, though, would hardly help, for it includes a House still to be elected by first-past-the-post.

76 Before the war, *"27% of marriages were mixed,"* **Thompson,** p 91, and *"of 150,000 Serbs in Sarajevo, 90,000 stayed with the Muslim majority and Croatian minority to face and fight what they called the fascist siege."* Ed **Vulliamy** in **The Guardian,** 10.2.94

77 In Bosnia's referendum, *"63% voted; of these, 99% voted [yes]. The great majority of Serbs, (31% of the population) boycotted"* the poll. **Thompson,** p 319.

INDEX

"*If I could not go to heaven but with a [political] party, I would not go there at all.*"

President Thomas Jefferson

"*The whole English constitution was arranged so that men might quarrel.*"

Lord Balfour

By the same author:

"Northern Ireland - That Sons May Bury Their Father", 1979,
   ISBN 0 906676 00 2

"Consensus - Democracy without opposition"* Moscow News, No 6/89

"Consensus"*, *"Novy Mir"*, [Russia], No 3/90

"Power, the psychology and politics of consensus"*, *"Pravo i Vlast"*,
Progress Publishers, Moscow, 1990,
   ISBN 5 01 003214 7

"Not by the majority alone", *"Debaty"* [Bulgaria], No 17/90

"A Bosnian Perspective", December Publications, 1993,
   ISBN 0 9517068 3 7

                  * *with my co-author, Irina Bazileva*

And on a different theme:

"Inflation? Try a Bicycle", the story of an 8,000 mile cycle ride in
Central Africa, 1978,
   ISBN 0 9506028 0 9

"The Dove of peace a'learning how to fly", some poetry from a
peace camp,
   ISBN 0 9506028 1 7

"What an extraordinary Title for a Travel Book", a comparison of
western European and African eco-systems, 1986,
   ISBN 0 9506028 2 5